The SLUMS of 1

Is Eternal Torment in Hell Biblical?

Erik Haglund

CONTENTS

INTRO: A LIVING HELL? 9

CHAPTER 1:   HE WHO GOES TO HELL FOR PASTIME 19

CHAPTER 2:   THE PLACE OF THE DEAD 30

CHAPTER 3:   ALL HELLS BREAK LOOSE 41

CHAPTER 4:   THE HISTORY OF HELL 57

CHAPTER 5:   TOO MANY IRONS IN THE FIRE 67

CHAPTER 6:   BOW TO THE KING 78

CHAPTER 7:   NOT A CHANCE IN HELL 86

CHAPTER 8:   DEAD MEN TELL NO TALES 96

CHAPTER 9:   REVELATION IN THE REVELATION 104

CHAPTER 10:   PAVED WITH GOOD INTENTIONS 115

CHAPTER 11:   THE BURNING QUESTION 126

CHAPTER 12:   THE REASON HE CALLS IT THE LAST DAY 142

CHAPTER 13:   TIME WON'T LET ME 152

CHAPTER 14:   PRIEST OR BEAST 174

APPENDIX A: THE ETERNITY WITH A BEGINNING 193

BIBLIOGRAPHY: 206

"It was with great enthusiasm that I read *The Slums of Heaven* and was thrilled with the well thought out presentation and Biblical conclusions. I highly recommend this work to anyone who is serious about studying the Word of God."

> Richard Oliver
> *The River International Network*

"Erik Haglund is a faithful student of the Word, willing to accept the truth that is revealed. Here Erik has well researched the controversial subjects around humanity's eternal dwelling place, a subject that needs to be rethought. I appreciate the work he has put into this topic and hope everyone will seriously consider his conclusions. Thank you, Erik, for your work."

> Dr. Harold R. Eberle
> *Author and President of Worldcast Ministries*

"Erik really has a passion for the word of God to be 'rightly divided'. In the pages of *The Slums of Heaven*, he does an awesome job of capturing a biblical look at the subject of Hell, and exposes the false doctrines that are out there. This is a book to grab your heart, give you compassion for hurting people, and it's a warning for humanity that there is a heaven to gain and a hell to shun!"

> Tom Scarrella
> *Tom Scarrella Ministries*

"Erik presents a case that is both challenging and compelling as he invites readers into an engaging examination of both Scripture and history. Regardless of what side of the argument you begin or end on, you will be better off for having read this thought-provoking book!"

> Pastor Mike Stehr
> *author, blogger*

INTRODUCTION:

A LIVING HELL?

"Honey, watch for cars," I remind my youngest daughter.

It's a warm breezy Saturday in this modest Minnesota town.

My family takes the sun-dappled sidewalk, and stops.

There it is again.

In the distance, I faintly hear a man's voice bellowing down the street, over the sound of traffic and birdsong.

I frown thinking, *'Fender bender?* That guy does not sound happy.'

The urgent voice drones on.

I detect a word here and there, *"...sin... death..."*

"Hmm," I turn to my wife, "Wanna go check this out?"

As we stroll into the open air of Town Square, the volume peaks.

Definitely no problem hearing every word now.

A bearded young man stands on a wooden crate, Bible in hand.

Neatly and soberly, he rattles off verses about the depravity of man, the plan of salvation, the Judgment to come. He's hoarse.

An older gentleman with a serious face pivots my way, and hands me a tightly folded little tract.

Words leap off the paper in black and white:

"WILL YOU BURN IN HELL FOREVER?"

I'm just home from work, and I check my messages.

A friend and avowed atheist has shared a meme on social media that keeps my gaze.

Perched atop a pile of naked human beings, demons hunch over the writhing mass.

The artist is good. Their faces belie agony.

A hideous creature plunges a trident into one man, screaming in anguish.

Fires rage in the background.

The text, in bold letters:

"GOD CREATED THIS PLACE FOR YOU TO BE TORTURED FOREVER-BECAUSE HE LOVES YOU."

I scroll past.

My wife and I emerge from a restaurant with some friends. It's a crisp still evening.

As weekend nightlife goes, not terribly busy. Couples saunter by the crosswalk.

Down on the corner, two fellows hold broad signs aloft, nicely printed in sharp letters.

Again, the words aren't hard to miss:

"WILL YOU RISK ETERNITY IN HELL?"

I like this guy on the radio. I'm feeling a little sorry for him about now, though.

After a noticeable pause, he lets out a nervous chuckle.

"That's a tough one," admits his co-host, an honest statement, and it buys the pastor the few seconds he needs.

That's time enough for a professional, as this man is.

Even so, this is one of the nastiest curve balls I've heard thrown in the popular radio Bible program.

And by a nine year old boy.

"How will we be happy in heaven, when some people we love will burn forever in Hell?"

After clearing his throat, the host assures all of us that God is just, and all-knowing. It's really for the best.

He concludes with something about God's sovereignty, and the punishment of evil.

All in all, nothing I disagree with.

He gives a good looking swing at the boy's pitch. There's solid truth in his reply.

As they move onto the next question, I get the feeling that he thinks he's knocked it out of the park. So do millions of people listening on their radios, I imagine.

I disagree. He nicked it foul, or walked, at best.

You see- he never answered the question.

CROSS EXAMINATION

That's exactly what we're going to cross-examine in this book.

I say *cross*-examine because after having studied multiple books from each biblical position on Hell, and first and foremost the Bible itself, I have questions for all sides.

Everything from Rob Bell's *Love Wins* (basically, *'Everyone will be saved from Hell, without exception'*) to Francis Chan's evangelical response *Erasing Hell* (basically, *'The unsaved will almost certainly burn in torment forever'*) I have given a serious hearing.

Without giving too much away, I'll only say that I assert that the truth lies somewhere in between.

What is Hell?

Is there any resemblance to the myths we've heard?

Who goes to Hell?

Will they burn in torment forever?

TO HELL AND GONE

A confession.

When I was first presented with an alternate view of Hell as I knew it, I felt a range of emotions.

First, skepticism.

With about the same faith I might mail in my winning sweepstakes number, I agreed to take a look at a recommended resource.

It can be a touchy subject.

In younger days, I frowned on conscientious objectors of Eternal Torment as naïve or backsliding.

Fast forward twenty years.

Was that a twinge of guilt I felt as I opened that first book with a view different than my own?

I think so.

I was reminded of the Berean Christians, **'more noble than those in Thessalonica, in that they received the word with all readiness of mind, *and* searched the scriptures daily, whether those things were so.'** Ac 17.11

What if Apollos had been intimidated by the many opponents of Paul, or declined Priscilla and Aquila as **'they took him aside, and explained to him the way of God more accurately'**?

After all, he was **'an eloquent man, and mighty in the scriptures.'**

Ac 18.24-26

He might have assumed he had nothing more to learn.

THE REAL DEAL

Third- there was a thin strand of hope.

It should be stated for the record that I myself have been perfectly willing to, and have accepted for well over twenty five years the thesis of conscious torment in eternal Hellfire.

And here I was being challenged with another perspective.

In our courts of law, if a case of reasonable doubt is made, the Judge takes this under advisement.

Is this not an indescribably heavier issue, worth a second look?

After prayer and careful study of resources from each perspective, I have come to a conclusion. The outcome of that is presented in this work for your consideration.

Ask yourself.

Is it at all possible that the Church may have been steered even slightly off-course in regard to what we've been taught about Hell, or any doctrine for that matter?

If you've studied Church history at any length, you already know the answer to that.

Literal millions of people have given **'heed to fables'** (1 Ti 1.4) in simple obedience to what they believed to be the will of God.

In point of fact, I will demonstrate here just where the champions stumbled, as the baton was passed from century to century.

ALL THE NEWS THAT'S FIT TO PRINT?

The street preacher.

The tract dealer.

The sign holder.

All sincere fellows, with the best intentions.

I love these people! I deeply honor their dedication. We can all take a lesson.

At the same time, would it be fair to take a second look at our approach to broken people who desperately want and need to believe that God loves them?

Many are at an emotional impasse with God.

They think that a deity who assigns billions of people to eternal torture is too cruel to approach. And yet the penalty for not approaching Him will be that very eternal torture.

We will always encounter folks wondering what humanity's eternal destiny is, if not heaven.

And then of course, the many who presume everyone is going to heaven also deserve the plain truth.

To be clear, it's not my aim to stir up controversy.

At the same time, it seems to me that it should bother us when error is loosely repeated in the Church.

Untaught hearers absorb the error. It spills over to their hearers, and so it goes. Something in me aches when I hear God misrepresented. I know He's used to it. I pick my battles.

Inevitably, the Holy Spirit groans in us as teachers to clear away the messes men have made on the foundation of His House.

I'm not sure I want to come to the place where we're willing to look on as a regime of bad theology is allowed to hold a seat **'in the house of God, which is the church of the living God, the pillar and ground of the truth.'**   1 Ti 3.15

FEARLESS VISION OR VISIONLESS FEAR

Near the close of the Dark Ages stood a host of men known as the Reformers.

What was it they hoped to reform?

As the Word of God came loose from its shackles of Latin ritualism, men began to read it in their own tongues.

The enormous divide between the Church of the 1st century and the Church of their day was becoming painfully clear.

Some called the Reformers misguided fools, only trying to wiggle out of mandatory attendance of the Mass, and the payment of indulgences.

Others believed that they were just passionate men who dared to unearth precious truths buried beneath slabs of religious tradition.

In any case, imagine if men such as Luther and Zwingli and Knox had looked at the extra-biblical religious machine churning over men's minds (and bodies, for that matter), and shrugged off the unpleasant thought of a dispute.

What if they had winced and shrunk back into the shadow of the immense power structure of Rome, and agreed to be quiet while the Church was being steered towards a cliff more cavernous than any in earth?

They could not.

Something inside compelled them to stand for truth, even into territory that cost many of them their families, fortunes, homes and lives.

To be clear, I believe that there are certain areas of doctrine that God may have left in shadow, not meant to be presumed with absolute assurance.

This may be one of those areas.

There are some who have charged we who dare to examine all sides of this as hiding our heads in the sand.

We've been accused of scrambling to avoid the harsh truth of God's wrath, judgment, etc...

On the contrary, can those who are willing to examine more evidence be accused of wanting to see less?

We can actually solve this mystery through prayerful examination of the biblical text, and church history.

By the end of this book, we'll either:

1) find the case groundless and dismiss it *or...*

2) may come to learn something long buried and hidden.

Each one of us must make that decision for ourselves.

CHAPTER 1:

'HE WHO GOES TO HELL FOR PASTIME'

A nervous gentleman stood before the gates of heaven, hat in hand.

He swallowed as St. Peter strolled out from the gates, unsure where his eternal home might be.

"Ah, *Carl*," Peter's eyes scoured the broad old parchment in his hands, "... here it is. *Carl Barnes.*"

The man brightened hearing his name.

Peter looked him over, "Unfortunately, you don't have the green light just yet. You're on a provisional list, it looks like."

The hair on the back of Carl's neck stood up.

Peter nodded as he studied the scroll, "Just a formality, really."

He turned to one of the angels standing in the white mist, "Please accompany Mr. Barnes on the grand tour."

"*Um...*" Barnes stuttered, motioning to the Pearly Gates, "if we're not going in *there*, what is this tour *of?*"

"Hell."

The angel was already moving towards the elevator doors, "We will walk into the outer regions of Hell. You can decide whether or not you want to stay there, or come back up here."

"Hmm," Carl followed him into the elevator, "That doesn't sound too bad, I guess."

After what seemed like an eternity, a bell finally dinged as the elevator slowed and rested to a stop.

With a mechanical sigh, the doors parted. Carl braced himself.

To his surprise, a refreshing breeze welcomed them.

Rather than the darkness and screams he was expecting, the mouth of Hell looked to roll out into the fairway of an extraordinary golf course.

The sun appeared to be shining. Birds were singing.

"Where are the demons?" Carl stepped out cautiously, "Who are those people down there by the clubhouse?"

"Those are actually a few of your buddies," the angel floated across the beautifully manicured green, "They've been waiting for you."

Wide-eyed, Carl hurried after him.

The buddies greeted him with smiles, and presented him with a cold beer, and an exceptional set of clubs.

After a fairly impressive nine holes, they retired to the air-conditioned dining room, where more drinks were served, along with some kind of incredible shrimp hor d'oeuvres brought by the host himself.

"These are superb," Carl wiped his mouth, "Can we get some more of these?"

"Certainly, sir," the host smiled, and removed a couple of dishes.

"Thanks, Satan," Jerry managed through an enormous mouthful of deviled egg.

Carl's fork clanked against his plate. He coughed, *"What* did you call him? Were you talking to the host?"

"Yeah. He does a good job here," Mike swilled the last of his drink.

Carl craned his neck towards the kitchen area, *"Really?* I always thought he was... meaner. And uglier."

"I know, right? Well... *you ready for nine more holes, buddy?"* Jerry pushed his chair back as the waitress brought another round, "The prime rib should be about done when we get back in. You like it medium rare, right?"

Carl grinned. He was feeling pretty good about now, "You're damned right."

Turning with a sheepish glance to the angel standing by, Carl belched, "I'll just stay behind, if it's all the same to you."

Realizing the angel said nothing, Carl waved him off as an afterthought, along with the busboy, "You guys can go."

The angel did not move, "Not without you, Carl Barnes."

Carl froze for a moment.

"Wha...? You said I could choose. I choose *Hell."*

'That is your choice,' the angel began to glide towards the door, "Follow me, and we will get it confirmed by the King."

"All the way up *there? Again?"* Carl's brow creased as he brushed some crumbs off of his shirt, "Just let Him know I'm good down here. I don't want to trouble you with an extra trip, you know."

"It will not take long," the angel paused in the doorway.

"Ugh," Carl tossed his napkin onto the tablecloth with a heavy sigh, "I'll be back as quick as I can, fellas."

It was quick indeed.

In no time, the order was approved and Carl was escorted back into the elevator. Slowly, the angel wafted into the recess.

Carl looked from the angel, to his watch and to the control panel, "Can we get this show on the road?" He motioned to the control panel, "Can I...?"

The angel nodded.

There were only two buttons. Carl stabbed the button with the arrow pointing 'down', and shifted uncomfortably, "Sorry. Tee time is in, like-three minutes."

Again, the angel was silent. The conveyor plummeted, this time with dreadful speed. As the bell dinged, the doors withdrew.

Carl's mind reeled.

A clammy horrid stench invaded his senses, as he looked out over the dark chasm sprawling with garbage.

And there was Jerry and the others, now dressed in oily rags, stooping to pick up trash.

As he was about to turn back to the elevator, a hideous man took him by the arm, "You can start over here. Put this on."

A greasy torn smock slapped wetly against his golf shirt.

Carl shuddered, looking narrowly at the awful man.

Ah! He recognized him now, without his serving jacket.

It was Satan himself!

"What happened to the greens? The clubhouse? You *lied* to me!"

Satan smiled, "A minute ago, I was just recruiting. Now, you're *staff.*"[1]

NOT A HOPE IN HELL

How many anecdotes do you suppose are floating around out there about Hell?

Whether humor or legend, there's no shortage of opinion.

As in the story above, one brags about the party in Hell with their friends, while the other claims there is no afterlife at all, much less in *Hell*.

They insist they'll take their last breath and decompose- end of story.

Another will point to the art and literature of the Dark ages.

Here, Hell is often portrayed as a massive subterranean torture chamber where people are immersed in pools of blood or human waste, while demons impale them with hot pitchforks.

Yet another urges that Hell is on earth, in the pain and injustice we inflict on one another.

Some like Origen believed that Hell was really a place of brief mortal suffering where our souls are 'cleaned up' before we stand before God.

C.S. Lewis seemed to think that Hell resembled a city of gloom where 'being fades away into nonentity'.[2]

And did you know that Christianity doesn't have the only or earliest version of Hell?

HUNG BY THE TONGUE

Among the oldest traditions of torment after death is the Hindu *Yama Pura*, a labyrinth of 21 main hells, and hundreds of thousands of lesser ones, 'worlds of nauseating disgusts, of loathsome agonies, of intolerable terrors'.

There, we are assured of iron spikes and 'dreadful shrieking'.

Some are hanged by the tongue, waiting to be eaten or whipped by venomous snakes.

Others are forced to swallow bowls of gore, hair and decayed matter, which are refilled the moment they finish!

The ancient Egyptian 'Book of the Dead' has long warned people of burning in blazing pits by 'the Commander of Fire', to then be cut into pieces by 'the Eater of Entrails'.

Islamic tradition predicts that infidels are to be hung over a furnace as their flesh is stripped off with scissors of fire, until all is peeled away, like insects shedding their skin.

The only thing to drink is scalding water.[3]

Not to be outdone, Buddhist *'Hells'* (over 40,000 of them) promise demons will be escorting sinners to the cauldrons and roasting spits upon death.

For those who see that as too predictable, another fate said to await us there is the removal of the skullcap, whereupon *hedgehogs*, of all things, will be shoved into the brain cavity.

Why so many and varied tortures here?

A specific Hell is set aside for each specific sin, everything from selling chickens at the wrong price to theft, to being nosy to eating sweets with rice.

UPSETTING THE SESAME SEED CART

With regard to eternity, Buddhist pupils are instructed to imagine a huge cart loaded with sesame seeds.

After one hundred years passes, the first seed is removed.

And as each century passes, one more seed is taken.

They are told that when *that* cart is finally empty, they will pass through that Hell to the next of thousands of Hells beyond it with... you guessed it. A *new cart* piled with sesame seeds. [4]

These views actually make the commonly held 'Christian' Hell look amateur!

In any case, our study here will begin and end with the Bible.

Inasmuch as this mystery can be understood, it will only be in God's word that we find reliable wisdom to guide us.

And there is a lot there, if we're willing to go after it.

1, 2, 3... GO!

There are three major biblical positions on *Hell* and its end result.

One of these is known as Universal Reconciliation or simply *Universalism.* Its proponents make the case that every human being on earth (past, present and future) will be received into heaven, after having gone through a time of purification in Hellfire, if necessary.

Another view is known as *Annihilation* or Conditional Immortality (*Conditionalism*). These advocate the view that those who reject the Lord Jesus Christ will at a given time simply be reduced to nothing in Hellfire, and cease to exist.

Far and away the most widely held view in Christendom is that of Eternal Torment, which contends that those who have not received Christ will be thrown into Hellfire to be tortured in conscious agony for eternity.

Each position has able proponents, and each lays claim to doctrinal accuracy.

So what better way to find our bearings than by the compass of scripture?

And we may as well begin with the word *Hell* itself.

TAKE IT TO THE GRAVE

Our English word 'Hell' is translated from the Hebrew *sheol*, and from the Greek *hades* (among others we'll touch on later).

A good example of this is shown in the following passages.

'For You will not abandon my soul to *Sheol*;
Nor will You allow Your Holy One to undergo decay'   Ps 16.10 NASB

About a thousand years later Luke records Peter's preaching... in Greek.

'BECAUSE YOU WILL NOT ABANDON MY SOUL TO *HADES*,

Nor allow Your Holy One to undergo decay.'   Ac 2.27 NASB

Our word *Hell* is descended from the Old English *helan*, and simply means 'to conceal, or to cover'.

This is what's meant in early literature when folks were *helling* their potatoes (storing them in a cellar) or *helling* the house with a thatched roof.

Linguist James Strong (yep, of the Concordance) defines *sheol* as 'the world of the dead' (the *hidden* place where the dead are held).

Understandably, many took this to mean **'the grave'**, as a place where the dead are 'hidden'.

But theologian W.E. Vine pointed out that *sheol* (286) is never used in reference to a literal tomb or grave. That's the Hebrew word *qeber* (keh`-ber).

So who exactly was Dr. Vine reminding of this?

As it turned out, Church leaders (in the Western hemisphere primarily) had, for a few hundred years, been basing their doctrine of *Hell* on the text of the King James Authorized Version.

As a regular reader of the King James, let me be openly honest. The translators (and their work) in 1611 emerged from a deeply legalistic and barbaric tone set by the Roman Church through the Dark Ages.

We'll look more closely at this later.

But as the word evolved over time and theology, *Hell* had come to mean not just the place where *all* the dead were awaiting the Judgment Seat of Christ, but a place where *only the wicked* souls were afflicted with unbearable torment until that time.

And the distinctions between '*Hell*' and **'the lake of fire'** (Re 19.20; 20.10,14-15) had blurred altogether.

Are they different?

We'll look into that shortly.

FIRE IN THE SHEOL!

The Hebrew word *sheol* appears in the Old Testament 66 times.

Instead of handling each consistently though, translators approached this dilemma by rendering *sheol* as *Hell* 32 times, when the wicked were clearly described.

'The wicked shall be turned into *hell*, and all the nations that forget God.'   Ps 9.17

When the *righteous* were the subject (31 times), the translators went with 'the grave'.

Hezekiah mourned, **'I said in the cutting off of my days, I shall go to the gates of the grave: I am deprived of the residue of my years.'**   Is 38.10

In Genesis 37.35, Jacob says of Joseph, **'I will go down to *the grave* unto my son mourning.'**

In the NASB, *sheol* is wisely left untranslated, as when Job lamented, **'Oh that You would hide me in *Sheol*, that You would conceal me until Your wrath returns to You.'**   Jb 14.13

THE SLUMS of HEAVEN

Here, it would appear that Job was *begging* for Hell!

Each of these are *sheol*.

But early translators were motivated by a mindset that was clearly reinforced by their calculated pick-and-choose. What was their error then?

It became apparent to the casual reader that 'bad people' go to Hell, while 'good people' don't.

'But good people don't *go to Hell! Or at least* Christians *don't!'* someone will say.

Or do they?

CHAPTER 2:

THE PLACE OF THE DEAD

The tale is told of the three-headed hellhound Cerberus, massive dog-beast in the dark caverns of Hades.

It was said that even the gods feared it.

From its place at the edge of the River Styx it stood, its six blood-red eyes stared out across the enormous river of molten lava moving slowly by. No mortal dared cross it.

Those few who had tried had been sheared and wolfed down by long teeth that lined each gaping mouth.

And none could slay the beast from behind- its tail, a huge serpent.

Only one voyager was welcomed on this dim shore.

Nightly, the ghoul *Charon* would ferry his long boat of newly dead souls across the burning slag into what became known as 'the fifth circle of Hell'.

There, he left the dead to be escorted down into eternal torture.

Enter the 21st century.

CHARON'S OBOL

Have you ever heard of the old tradition of placing a coin in the mouth of the dead before burial?

Did you know that, until recently, many people still practiced this rite of *'Charon's obol'*?

Why?

Would you believe this was intended as boat fare for the deceased to give to the usher of Hell?

Astonishingly, some may still keep this tradition today.

Think about this.

How is it that intelligent people of days past were actually compelled to take part in this ritual, among other ancient lore?

Whether it be Cerberus, the chariot of hell, or haunting romantic tales from Dante and Milton, Greek mythology and English literature about the underworld can be morbidly interesting.

Over the centuries, these stories became interwoven with biblical truths either exaggerated or neglected.

And the hybrid became the inspiration for countless horrid depictions of God, and His place of the dead, what some call the outer darkness, the Slums of Heaven.

So- let's call God's own Word to the stand.

THE PLACE OF THE DEAD

'David says concerning Him… For You will not leave my soul in *Hades*, Nor will You allow Your Holy One to see corruption.' Ac 2.25-27

Here, Peter preaches Christ by the inspired word of David.

Evidently, Christ Himself was (briefly) in Hell or *hades*, 'the Place of the Dead'.

What exactly was He doing there?

**'Therefore He says: "When He ascended on high,
He led captivity captive,
And gave gifts to men."**

(Now this, "He ascended"—what does it mean but that He also first descended into the lower parts of the earth?

He who descended is also the One who ascended far above all the heavens, that He might fill all things)' Ep 4.8-10

THE LOWER PARTS OF THE EARTH

Here, Paul also cites David.

In Psalm 68, the Holy Spirit foretold Christ's descent **'into the lower parts of the earth'**, a doctrine known as *descensus ad infernos*.

Legions of Old Testament saints were loosed from their state, and led in a massive procession of souls **'on high'**.[5]

In a matter of days all of the righteous dead would follow Christ '**when he ascended up on high,** as 'He led captivity captive'.

In light of the traditional take on Hell that most of us have been taught, some may be wondering how God could have left many millions of good people to burn in Hellfire for hundreds, or thousands of years as the earth waited for Christ in **'the dispensation of the fullness of times.'**

Ep 1.10

Are we sure this torment in *sheol* before the Judgment seat of Christ is scripturally accurate?

PERISH THE THOUGHT

Let's take a peek at this passage:

Psalm 6.5, **'For there is no mention of You in death; In *Sheol* who will give You thanks?'**.

Why is God not spoken of in *sheol*?

Let's find out.

'The living know that they will die, but the dead *know nothing*; they have no more reward, and even the memory of them is lost...

Whatever your hand finds to do, do with your might; for there is *no work* or *thought* or *knowledge* or *wisdom* in *Sheol*, to which you are going.'   Ec 9.5,10

We notice here the inspired text announces that *every* soul hearing this is going to *sheol*.

Every soul is going to the place of the dead.

Psalm 146.4, **'His breath goes forth, he returns to his earth; in that very day *his thoughts perish.'***

Scripture is clear.

Every dead man has *'no work* or *thought* or *knowledge* or *wisdom* in *Sheol'*.

In death, he will *'know nothing'*.

In fact, **'his thoughts *perish.'***

DON'T MAKE ME COME DOWN THERE!

Psalm 115.17,18 (NRSV), **'The dead do not praise the Lord,
Nor *do* any who *go down into silence*;
18 But as for us** [the living]**, we will bless the Lord
From this time forth and forever.
Praise the Lord!'**

Psalm 31.17-18, **'Let me not be put to shame, O Lord, for I call upon**

You;
Let the wicked be put to shame, let them be silent in *Sheol*.

Let the lying lips be mute,
Which speak arrogantly against the righteous
With pride and contempt'.

Psalm 94.17, **'If the LORD had not been my help,**
My soul would soon have dwelt in the abode of *silence'*.

There doesn't appear to be any weeping, gnashing of teeth, screaming, etc... here in *sheol*.

It's described as a place they will **'be silent'**.

Why?

SLEEP ON IT

Psalm 13.3, **'Consider *and* answer me, O LORD my God;**
Enlighten my eyes, or I will sleep the *sleep of* death.'

This makes sense.

Silence is conducive to sleep.

Matthew 9.23-25, **'When Jesus came into the official's house, and**
saw the flute-players and the crowd in noisy disorder,

[24] He said, "Leave; for the girl has not died, but is asleep." And
they began laughing at Him.

35

[25] But when the crowd had been sent out, He entered and took her by the hand, and the girl got up'.

John 11.11-13, **'This He said, and after that He said to them, "Our friend Lazarus has fallen asleep; but I go, so that I may awaken him out of sleep."**

The disciples then said to Him, "Lord, if he has fallen asleep, he will recover."

Now Jesus had spoken of his death, but they thought that He was speaking of literal sleep'.

This metaphor is throughout the scriptures, of death as *sleep*.

Why?

It sounds like the souls of those who have died are at rest until **'the resurrection on the last day.'**   Jn 11.24

If this state of metaphysical sleep be the case, it would seem that conscious existence is suspended, as in physical sleep.

If this is true, this would explain why the dead do not cry, or curse, or think or suffer.

They await the **'great white throne and Him who sat upon it, from whose presence earth and heaven fled away, and no place was found for them.**

And I saw the dead, the great and the small, standing before the throne, and books were opened; and another book was opened, which is *the book* of life; and the dead were judged from the things which

were written in the books, according to their deeds.

And the sea gave up the dead which were in it, and death and Hades gave up the dead which were in them; and they were judged, every one *of them* **according to their deeds.**

Then death and Hades were thrown into the lake of fire. This is the second death, the lake of fire.'   Re 20.11-14

Also notice here that **'hell'** is thrown into **'the lake of fire'**.

It looks as if they may be two separate entities.

Now- I wonder if this next thought may be crossing your mind...

WHAT ABOUT MOSES AND ELIJAH?

'Moses and Elijah weren't asleep when Jesus talked with them at the Transfiguration,' someone points out.

A fair question.

At the same time, we notice that Christ described their appearance as a *vision,* **'Jesus charged them, saying, Tell the vision to no man, until the Son of man be risen again from the dead.'**   Mt 17.9

Is this a record of these actual prophets having spoken with Jesus, or was this a vision?

And if these *were* the actual men standing on earth for a moment again, could it be that they were called away from sleep, as Samuel seems to say?

'Samuel said to Saul: Why hast thou disturbed my rest...?' (1 Sam 28.13-15, DRA). The NLV has, **'"Why have you troubled my rest by bringing me up?"'**

These versions seem to say that Samuel was disturbed from *rest.*

What kind of rest?

Did God permit them to 'wake up' for this quick assignment?

Or do the righteous dead no longer sleep, after the Ascension, as per Ephesians 4.8-10?

God knows.

After having examined texts in support of either view, I'm not sure I can say either emerges as absolutely conclusive.

But the next section should bring some clarity.

KILLING ME SOFTLY

Isaiah had some hard words for the King of Babylon.

Some of you may be reminded of the dead men who spoke to the king of Babylon in *sheol*, in Isaiah 14.9-11:

'Sheol from beneath is excited over you to meet you when you come; It arouses for you the spirits of the dead, all the leaders of the earth; It raises all the kings of the nations from their thrones.
10 "They will all respond and say to you,
'Even you have been made weak as we,

You have become like us.
[11] 'Your pomp *and* the music of your harps
Have been brought down to Sheol;
Maggots are spread out *as your bed* beneath you
And worms are your covering.'

To the naked eye, this does seem to be a convincing text for conscious torment in *sheol*.

Men here appear to be moving around and speaking in Hell.

We need to be reminded that this passage is an example of what is known as *apocalyptic symbolism*, a specific poetic tone expressed by the Holy Spirit throughout the prophets.

One reason we know this to be the case here is by its context.

Notice verse 8 directly before this:

"Even the cypress trees rejoice over you, *and* the cedars of
Lebanon, *saying*,
'Since you were laid low, no *tree* cutter comes up against us.'

Obviously trees aren't rejoicing or talking here, any more than these men are.

These are dead men expressed in ancient poetic language as we've covered, **'there is… no thought or knowledge or wisdom in *sheol*… the dead know nothing.'**   Ec 9.10,5

This is apocalyptic symbolism, used to convey great universal concepts visually, like a parable.

THE SLUMS of HEAVEN

This is God's prophetic omen to the king of Babylon that the leaders of nations who remain after his death will no longer fear him, and that he will be crushed and reduced to the level of every other man at death.

The mention that **'maggots are spread out *as your bed* beneath you, and worms are your covering'** (v. 11) is also interesting, as maggots and worms don't feed on the living but on corpses.

This is plainly symbolic of death.

And what other concept is shown in the imagery of **'your bed... your coverings'**?

That of *sleep.*

Another passage dealing with *sheol* is Ezekiel 32.17-32, where God describes the conquest of Egypt by the Chaldeans, and the hordes of men who will be **'killed by the sword.'**   v.20

He reveals their descent into *sheol*, **'to the world below'** (v.18) to join the countless dead warriors of Elam, Assyria, Edom, etc...

In the course of these fifteen verses, we don't read of any writhing, screaming, burning, gnashing of teeth, etc...

What we do see described is that they are **'laid to rest'** (v.19), **'they lie still'** (v.21) in **'a bed'** (v.25), as they **'lie among the uncircumcised'** (v.28), **'lie with the uncircumcised'** (v.29), **'they lie uncircumcised with those who are killed by the sword'** (v.30), and are **'laid to rest.'**   v.32

Death is a long sleep as **'they lie still'** until **'the resurrection on the last day.'**   Jn 11.24

But believe it or not, we still have *two more* 'Hells' to quickly touch on!

CHAPTER 3:

ALL HELLS BREAK LOOSE

'And though this world, with demons fill'd,

Should threaten to undo us,

We will not fear, for God hath willed

His truth to triumph through us.

The Prince of darkness grim,

We tremble not for him;

His rage we can endure,

For lo, his doom is sure-

One little word shall fell him.'[6]

Amen, Luther!

As it turns out, there are a few less demons roaming the earth after their violation in Genesis 6.

That is a tricky discussion in itself.

But the fact remains- where were these supernatural lawbreakers put?

And how does one put a demon 'in jail'?

We've examined the Hebrew word *sheol* (in Greek- *hades*).

But did you know that there are two more Greek words translated as **'hell'** in our English versions?

They are *tartaro`o* (tar-tar-ah`-ho) and *gehenna*.

Let's look first at *tartaro`o.*

TARTARO'O

From it, we get the more commonly heard *Tartarus*, thought to be a subterranean place of torment, largely taken from Plato and other Greek philosophers.

There's just one occurrence of this word in the New Testament, found in 2 Peter 2.4:

'For if God spared not the angels that sinned, but cast them down to hell, and delivered them into chains of darkness, to be reserved unto judgment.'

There's disagreement among scholars on the most accurate rendering, as *tartaro`o* is here actually a *verb,* (to cast down), but was not translated as such.

Mounce's Reverse-Interlinear has,
'Forgar ifei ·ho Godtheos didpheidomai notou sparepheidomai the angel
sangelos when they

sinnedhamartanō butalla casttartaroō them into helltartaroō, committin
gparadidōmi them to chainsseira of utter darknesszophos,
there to be kepttēreō untileis the judgmentkrisis;

The NRSV footnotes **'hell'**, admitting this is simply an extrapolation of
the verb *tartaro`o*, as we see above.

Some translators weren't willing to make the leap to a word that just
isn't found in the original text, but only implied.

Hence, Darby has, **'For if God spared not [the] angels who had sinned,
but having cast them down *to the deepest pit of gloom* has delivered
them to chains of darkness [to be] kept for judgment.'**

The Common English Bible has, **'God didn't spare the angels when they
sinned but cast them into *the lowest level of the underworld* and
committed them to chains of darkness, keeping them there until the
judgment'**.

The demons that violated the metaphysical boundaries set by God in
Genesis 6.1-4 *were* put someplace 'hidden', as we're told. Agreed.

My bone to pick with this verse has more to do with the mutation Hell
underwent in the minds and pulpits of men through the Dark Ages.

Slowly, *Hell* morphed from the silent place of all human souls awaiting
resurrection to the loud chaotic horror show of gargoyles and broiling
torture often alleged today.

Mistranslations like these are partly responsible for that.

'But Jesus warned of worms and unquenchable fire, didn't He?'

He did. Let's look at that.

NOW WE'VE OPENED A CAN OF WORMS!

This actually brings us to our third Greek word for Hell- *gehenna*.

The most often used word in the New Testament for Hell, *gehenna* appears only twelve times.

James refers to *Hell* once, while Christ mentions it in the gospels on no more than four occasions.

Hell occurs nowhere in John's gospel.

The history behind *Gehenna* is fascinating.

Gehenna is actually taken from Gehinnom, or Ben-Hinnom, the Valley of the son of Hinnom, a ravine that slopes down away from the city of Jerusalem to the south and west.[7]

Today, it's known as *Wadi Jehennam* or *Wadi er Rubeb*.

As far back as the age of the kings, the Valley of Hinnom was notorious as a hive of pagan idolatry and human sacrifice, especially the murder of children in worship to Molech.

The shrine set up in *Gehenna* was *Topheth*, meaning 'drum' for the beating of drums during ritual sacrifice of infants to the Ammonite god.

One purpose for these drums was to drown out the cries of babies who were laid into the Molech's outstretched hands, superheated by fire lit within the bronze cattle-headed image.

Interestingly, kings Ahaz and Mannaseh burnt their own sons to death in worship of Molech, to seek favor from him.[8]

'So,' someone may be thinking, *'Is Jesus' mention of the worms and fire of Gehenna nothing more than a nod to southwest Jerusalem's wrong side of the tracks?'*

Not at all.

Whether wheat fields or wells, trees or towers, Jesus constantly used the common things around Him to illustrate deeper realities.

Let's begin with what we likely agree on.

In the text we're about to examine, Jesus used *Gehenna* as a metaphor for final judgment, that **'whosoever was not found written in the book of life was cast into the lake of fire.'** Re 20.15

Agreed.

What the finer points of that will look like are debatable. I think we can all agree that it will be indescribably bad for those who reject Jesus to the bitter end.

Here's the passage in question:

WHERE THE WORM DOES NOT DIE

'And if your hand offend you, cut it off: it is better for you to enter into life maimed, than having two hands to go into hell [gehenna], **into the fire that never shall be quenched:**

[44] Where the worm does not die, and the fire is not quenched.

[45] And if your foot offend you, cut it off: it is better for you to enter

into life lame, than having two feet to be cast into hell [gehenna], into the fire that never shall be quenched:

⁴⁶ Where the worm does not die, and the fire is not quenched.

⁴⁷ And if your eye offend you, gouge it out: it is better for you to enter into the kingdom of God with one eye, than having two eyes to be cast into hell [gehenna] fire:

⁴⁸ Where the worm does not die, and the fire is not quenched'

Mk 9.43-48

Let's look at this as it would have been heard by those deeply traditional 1ˢᵗ century Jews, held by ancient roots of meaning thousands of years old.

First, the word Jesus uses here is *gehenna* (the actual physical valley beside the city) and not *hades* nor *tartaro'o*.

This word is certainly well-known by His hearers, imagery of the Judgment to come.

On this I'm sure we agree.

But are we now to understand then that there will be immortal worms that will feed on writhing screaming human beings for eternity?

I question that.

Actually, in regard to the wicked at the Judgment, **'the moth shall eat them up like a garment, and the worm shall eat them like wool: but my righteousness shall be forever, and my salvation from generation to generation.'**

Is 51.8

The Holy Spirit as much as concludes it is not insects that last forever.

He adds, **'But my righteousness will be forever'** (as opposed to these worms, or the dead they feed on).

This is apocalyptic imagery, and not likely a prophecy of immortal worms.

And consider:

If we accept the part about our hacking our own limbs from our bodies and gouging out our own eyes as symbolic, why must the worms be seen as literal?

I commend Francis Chan's honest assessment of this passage.

He writes, 'In Isaiah's context, the worm doesn't die as it eats the flesh of dead bodies. There's nothing in the context that says the souls of the dead are still being tormented. The image of worms feasting on unburied dead people emphasizes the shame of defeat.'[9]

A HOT TIME IN THE OLD TOWN TONIGHT

Did you happen to notice the name of another prophet in relation to our passage above?

Did you know that Jesus wasn't the first to use the phrase **'fire that is not quenched'**?

Jesus was actually citing *Isaiah,* where we read, **'And they shall go out and look at the dead bodies of those who have rebelled against me, for their worm shall never die; their fire shall not be quenched; and they shall be a disgusting sight to all mankind.'**   Is 66.24

In its context, Isaiah 66 is an indictment of ritualistic Judaism:

'Whoever sacrifices a bull is like one who kills a person, and whoever offers a lamb is like one who breaks a dog's neck; whoever makes a grain offering is like one who presents pig's blood, and whoever burns memorial incense is like one who worships an idol. They have chosen their own ways, and they delight in their abominations.'

So the Jewish people had fallen into a pattern of dead ritual.

Does this bring to mind any resemblance to other passages?

'But if you do not listen to Me to keep the sabbath day holy by not carrying a load and coming in through the gates of Jerusalem on the sabbath day, then I will kindle a fire in its gates and it will devour the palaces of Jerusalem and not be quenched'　　　Jeremiah 17.27

'not be quenched'?

Is there a literal fire still burning today at the gates of Jerusalem for their disobedience?

No.

This is apocalyptic symbolism for a brutal judgment that was not rescinded.

What exactly was that judgment?

In 605 B.C., about four years after King Josiah died, the Chaldeans crushed Egypt at the battle of Carchemish (see Je 46.2).[10]

Despite Jeremiah's bellows, the people refused to listen, even as Nebuchadnezzar's forces raged towards the Holy Land.

Babylon's first incursion into the city came that same year, with tens of thousands of captives exiled- and executed.

By 586 B.C., Jerusalem, its temple and all Judea were a desolate smoking ruin.[11]

This is the symbolic meaning of **'unquenchable fire'**.

THE FLAME THAT WILL NOT BE QUENCHED

Now let's see if Ezekiel has anything to add.

'The word of the LORD came to me:

"Son of man, set your face toward the south; preach against the south and prophesy against the forest of the southland.

Say to the southern forest: 'Hear the word of the LORD. This is what the Sovereign LORD says: I am about to set fire to you, and it will consume all your trees, both green and dry. The blazing flame will not be quenched, and every face from south to north will be scorched by it.

Everyone will see that I the LORD have kindled it; it will not be quenched.'   20.45-48

'The blazing flame will not be quenched'?

Was **'every face'**, every living person consumed by eternal fire?

They were not.

It's also interesting that the text doesn't say *'preach against the whole earth, and prophesy imminent hell for all the people who reject God'*, but a region, simply **'the southland.'**

One region.

Is there now a literal fire still burning across southern Judea (where Jerusalem is situated) for their disobedience?

No.

This is apocalyptic symbolism for a brutal judgment that was not rescinded.

So what exactly was Ezekiel prophesying here?

He was himself also taken captive and dragged back into Babylon in irons (from southern Judea, as the prophecy warns) during Babylon's conquest.

Once again, the Holy Spirit speaks in parables and prophetic mystery to those who will hear.

Unfortunately, most didn't listen.

THE HELL YOU SAY

Now let's let Jeremiah weigh in.

He was frighteningly blunt.

'Because they have filled this place with the blood of the innocent and have built the high places of Baal to burn their sons in the fire as burnt offerings to Baal, a thing which I never commanded or spoke of, nor did it ever enter My mind.'

Remember our little history lesson on the pagans of *Topheth?*

Jeremiah goes on.

'Therefore, behold, days are coming," declares the LORD, "when this place will no longer be called Topheth or the valley of Ben-hinnom, but rather the valley of Slaughter.

I will make void the counsel of Judah and Jerusalem in this place, and I will cause them to fall by the sword before their enemies and by the hand of those who seek their life; and I will give over their carcasses as food for the birds of the sky and the beasts of the earth.

I will also make this city a desolation and an object of hissing; everyone who passes by it will be astonished and hiss because of all its disasters.

I will make them eat the flesh of their sons and the flesh of their daughters, and they will eat one another's flesh in the siege and in the distress with which their enemies and those who seek their life will distress them."' 19.4-9

God's dark omen from the mouth of the prophet came horribly true.

THE HORDES OF BABYLON

In 589 B.C., the hordes of Babylon swarmed the holy city in a brutal 30-month siege.

Finally, after literally ripping down sections of the immense stone wall, they poured in.

At his arrest, king Zedekiah was made to watch as his sons were slaughtered.

It would be the last thing he saw. His captors then put out his eyes, and dragged him blinded and bound into the Chaldean dungeons.

Truly, "every worst woe befell the city, which drank the cup of God's fury to the dregs."[12]

THEIR CORPSES

Now we can understand this symbolism in context, as the *International Bible Commentary* advises, 'There is no doctrine of hell in the Old Testament. In Isaiah 66:24, at one time a much quoted verse, the reference is not to the continuing personality (*nephesh*) of the rebels, *but to their corpses*' (emphasis mine).[13]

It must also be brought to our attention that this phrase *Unquenchable Fire* was in common use elsewhere at these times.

From Homer's description of fatal Trojan assaults of 'unquenchable fire' on Grecian warships (*Iliad* 16.123,194) to Eusebius' account of the 'unquenchable fire' that broiled a martyr to ash (*Eccl. Hist.* 6.41).[14]

Of course these fires soon died out.

Fast forward six centuries.

Gehenna in Jesus' day was no less squalid.

Though king Josiah had **'defiled the Topheth in the Ben-hinnom Valley so no one could burn their child alive in honor of the god Molech'** (2 Ki 23.10), it was still a foul trash dump, crematorium, and toilet (literally).

EXCUSE ME, WHERE'S THE RESTROOM?

There are some today who brush off *Gehenna's* history as Jerusalem's literal cesspool/ landfill thick with stench, animal carcasses, human waste, rats and... yes. Maggots and smoldering fires.

I have heard a number of teachers claim that there is no evidence for this, only a diversion from Christ's preaching on eternal Hell.

The facts aren't actually difficult to find.

In 1997, Bargil Pixner discovered the Essene gate just uphill the valley of Hinnom.[15]

Why did the people of Jerusalem need a gate there?

Deuteronomy 23.12, **'designate a place outside the camp where you can go relieve yourself.'**

I'll spare you anymore detail than that.

This is the most basic logic, understood by people for thousands of years.

Does one relieve oneself uphill from where they live, or downhill?

The people certainly knew better than to **'designate a place'** up on the north side of the city. Their restroom was the valley of Hinnom, where waste travelled down away from their homes and water supply.

Pixner also discovered there the latrine system of the Essenes (by what is still known today as 'the dung gate', by the way).

We also have historical reference to fires in the Valley of Hinnom from ancient literature, such as that of Rabbi David Kimhi in his commentary on Psalm 27, about A.D. 1200.

The Jews took the same approach with *Gehenna* as their *garbage dump*.

And notice the topography of Jerusalem. This is important.

Built on a hill sloping south with its lowest point where the valley of Hinnom meets the Kidron Valley, they merge and grade down to the Dead Sea.

While the Jews were careful to bury their fellowman, animals were another matter.

In our modern age, it's so easy for us to forget the past vital role of livestock, beasts of burden and of course- *sacrificial* animals.

TAKING THE LOW ROAD

As closely tied to Jewish work and worship as these big beasts were, they weren't about to spend any time digging graves for carcasses often several hundred pounds of dead weight.

And yet, they couldn't leave them to decay and draw vermin and disease.

They'd have to be dragged away- and burned.

As a resident of Jerusalem in say, A.D. 10, imagine that one of your oxen dies.

Are you apt to try to drag it uphill, or down?

You drag it down to Hinnom and burn it.

If you're emptying your chamber pot into the archaic sewer system, you want it to carry *away* from your home, not back towards it.

We should also be reminded that even in Jesus' day, Jerusalem itself was home to well over 80,000 people- and all their animals.

They needed a place to take care of 'all of the above'. *Gehenna* was that place.

Today, guides in the Holy Land can show you the trenches where the remains of sacrificial beasts were burned, along with the garbage and waste.

And yet another grim use was made of *Gehenna*.

DEAD MAN'S CURVE

In an age where cities would come under siege from hostile armies, corpses would be thrown over the walls of the down slope to avoid disease in the city as they rotted (and in hope of repelling or infecting those outside).

It was just this carnage about which Jeremiah had prophesied.

After all, **'surely the Lord GOD will do nothing, but he reveal his secret unto his servants the prophets.'**   Am 3.7

Jesus also warned of imminent assault by Rome, as Jeremiah had also predicted the scourge of Chaldeans centuries earlier.

This unquenchable fire of judgment did come to Jerusalem in A.D. 70, this time a *Roman* torch in God's hand.

The great historian Josephus documented how corpses were indeed thrown over the walls into *Gehenna* when the besieged had nowhere else to dispose of the dead.[16]

So now we have touched on historical *Gehenna*.

At the same time, our perceptions have been shaped by some of the medieval depictions of *Hell*.

One graphically repulsive painting, for instance, has a leviathan eating and defecating out living human beings.

Is this really what we have to look forward to?

How have we come to some of these gruesome theories?

By Scripture?

Or by some other way?

CHAPTER 4:

THE HISTORY OF HELL

Imagine you're on a game show.

The host flashes a toothy smile and looks your way.

"Question:

Do a majority of people believe that Hell is a place of eternal torment in fire?"

You check your pool of earnings. It's up to $2000.

"Clock's ticking," the host chuckles pointlessly.

Duh. You already know that. It's all you can hear as you wait for the buzzer to squall.

Two buttons are lit up on your podium.

A big green *Yes* and a big red *No.*

Better hit one fast.

Which one?

SURVEY SAYS!

I'm willing to bet most of you would smack that green button.

And wager most or all of your money on it.

So would I.

Why not?

Isn't this as bedrock as any doctrine since the beginning of the Church?

Now suppose we ask a thousand Christians if we are saved by grace, or establish our faith on scripture alone.

I'd take those bets too.

We may collect even higher totals for those questions.

Why?

Because Dad or Grandma told us so?

Because the majority of Christians happen to believe it?

In point of fact, the doctrine of *Hell was* universally held by the early church.

The doctrine of *eternal torment,* on the other hand, was almost unheard of for the first three centuries, and very seldom regarded for the first *four* centuries.

TURN OF THE CENTURIES

Through this next section, we'll look briefly at six stages of worldview on Hell, in order of time:

1) the Old Testament,

2) the intertestamental period,

3) the teachings of Christ,

4) the teachings of Paul,

5) the remainder of the New Testament, including the Revelation, and

6) the history of the Church up to today.

Interestingly, we read from the Bible Gateway Encyclopedia:

'The teaching that there is a place where the ungodly are punished forever is scarcely mentioned in the OT. In the intertestamental period, however, this idea became prominent [especially among the Pharisees, the Essenes, etc...] although its acceptance by the rabbis was far from unanimous.'

With more than 13,000 articles, the Jewish Virtual Library has been defined as 'the most comprehensive online Jewish encyclopedia in the world'.

'Regarding the hereafter', JVL maintains, 'Jewish teachings on the subject of the afterlife are sparse: the Torah, the most important Jewish text, has no clear reference to afterlife at all.'[17]

JewFaq.org states, '[B]ecause Judaism is primarily focused on life here and now rather than on the afterlife, Judaism does not have much dogma about the afterlife, and leaves a great deal of room for personal opinion.'[18]

At this point, certain Old Testament proof texts may be coming to mind about now.

Let's take a fresh look at a few of those.

AS SURE AS HELL

Regarding humanity at the final Judgment, Daniel is told, **'And many of them that sleep in the dust of the earth shall awake, some to everlasting life, and some to shame and everlasting contempt.**

[3] And they that be wise shall shine as the brightness of the firmament; and they that turn many to righteousness as the stars for ever and ever'
                                                                 12.2-3

This text is often cited as proof of eternal torment.

But let's investigate more closely.

We begin by noticing that some are raised **'to everlasting life'**, while the others are not.

According to Romans chapter 8, the opposite of life is *death*.

Paul teaches **'For I am persuaded, that neither death, nor life, nor angels, nor principalities, nor powers, nor things present, nor things to come,**

Nor height, nor depth, nor any other creature, shall be able to separate us from the love of God, which is in Christ Jesus our Lord'

THE SLUMS of HEAVEN

Ro 8.38-39

Here, Paul has presented a list of antithetical realities.

We delve into Paul's doctrine in detail in Chapter 8, but at this point, let's take an honest deep breath.

Might it be fair to ask if the opposite of *life* may be something other than life in torment?

Might the opposite of existence be *nonexistence?*

John Locke stated bluntly, 'By death, some men understand endless torments in hell fire, but it seems a strange way understanding a law which requires the plainest and directest of words, that by death should be meant eternal life in misery".[19]

Because the crux of this verse lay in the original text, I'll footnote from the Hebrew interlinear for you [20] and simply ask you to mark my word.

And that word is... *oulm*.

This was the word translated here **'everlasting'**, and we blow away the fog surrounding this word in Chapter 13.

Hang on tight.

SWEATIN' TO THE OLDIES

I've had Traditionalists bring me to Isaiah:

'The sinners in Zion are afraid; Fearfulness has seized the hypocrites: "Who among us shall dwell with the devouring fire?   33.14

Indeed, who among us?

If asked by Isaiah, I might answer, "None. No one can dwell in it. It's a *'devouring* **fire'**.

They are devoured by the fire.

They are reduced to nothing.

They have chosen nonexistence.

Unlike the fire shown to Moses, when **'the angel of the LORD appeared unto him in a flame of fire out of the midst of a bush: and he looked, and, behold, the bush burned with fire, and the bush *was not consumed'** (Ex 3.2), this fire consumes, devours.

This is why no one can **'dwell'** in it.

They are swallowed up and extinguished in its force and fury.

Each of the three positions on the nature of Hell also holds its own view on **'the lake of fire'** and the purpose of this final fire.

WITHERED BRANCHES

Universalists see this fire as purifying and redemptive.

Traditionalists see this fire as regenerating and torturing.

Conditionalists see this fire as devouring and consuming.

Often, Christ used agricultural pictures of the disobedient as **'withered branches'** (Jn 15.6), **'useless weeds'** (Mt 13.40) or trees with bad fruit to be **'cut down and thrown into the fire.'**   Mt 7.19

We were not intended to see these metaphors as Moses' burning bush.

The meaning is plain enough.

Traditionalists tell us that the damned will be preserved, and not consumed in the last fire.

Christ tells us that they will be consumed, and not preserved, **'as the weeds are pulled up and burned in the fire, *so will it be* at the end of the age.'**

Mt 13.40

QUENCHABLE FIRE?

Did you know that Isaiah prophesied of **'unquenchable fire'** on more than one occasion?

'For *it is* the day of the LORD's vengeance,
The year of recompense for the cause of Zion.
9 Its streams shall be turned into pitch,
And its dust into brimstone;
Its land shall become burning pitch.
10 It shall not be quenched night or day;
Its smoke shall ascend forever.
From generation to generation it shall lie waste;
No one shall pass through it forever and ever'

Is 34.8-10

Are fires and streams of molten lava still burning in Edom (Idumea)?

No.

In the 6th century B.C., Edom was swallowed up and plundered by raging nomadic Arab tribes, as Isaiah warned. [21]

John Calvin also weighs in, 'The prophet's language is undoubtedly hyperbolical... When he declares that the wrath of God against the Edomites will resemble a fire of God that burns continually, he cuts off from them all hope of pardon'.[22]

Pardon?

Were there any fires of judgment that weren't unpardonable or 'unquenchable'?

Recall now the Exodus, when God told Moses His plan to destroy the new fledgling nation of Israel, several million people all at once.

'Now therefore, let Me alone, that My wrath may burn hot against them and I may consume them. And I will make of you a great nation.'

32.10

Yet we know that **'Moses besought the LORD his God... Turn from your fierce wrath.'**

He did.

God never described this fire as *unquenchable*.

This fire of judgment was quenched, and they were pardoned.

It wasn't long until the people had formed another coalition to oppose Moses, and **'when the LORD heard it, His anger was kindled, and the fire of the LORD burned among them and consumed some of the outskirts of the camp.**

The people therefore cried out to Moses, and Moses prayed to the LORD and the fire died out.'

Nu 11.1-2

Again, God never called this judgment *unquenchable*.

The fire was snuffed out, and they were pardoned.

LIKE A HOUSE ON FIRE

Traditionalists have also been known to go to the final prophet of the Old Covenant.

Malachi wrote:

'Certainly the day is coming! It will burn like a furnace. All arrogant people and all evildoers will be like straw. The day that is coming will burn them up completely," says the LORD of Armies. "It won't leave a single root or branch.' Ma 4.1

While those who love God are said to leap like calves released from the stall into the open meadow, the wicked are only described as **'ashes under the soles of your feet on the day which I am preparing.'** Ma 4.3

Malachi was told that the fire on the final day would consume the arrogant, leaving them **'neither root nor branch'**.

In scripture, the metaphor of the **'root'** and **'branch'** is an emblem of the *seen* (the branch) and the *unseen* (the root), most often in the language of *a surviving remnant.*[23]

This is also understood as the *body* (what is seen) and the *spirit* (what is unseen).

No one will disagree that here we read of the Day **'burning like a furnace'** and the wicked **'set... ablaze'**.

But the assertion that this must be interpreted as eternal torment is a bridge too far, I think. Neither duration nor eternity is mentioned.

If anything, we see here the *end* of the wicked **'tread down'** as **'ashes under the soles of your feet'**.

We're told that they will not be left **'root nor branch'**.

Nothing will be left.

It would seem that the body will not continue.

It would seem that the spirit will also not continue.

In this text, it appears that they will be *consumed* in this last fire.

Without any real 'smoking gun' in the Old Testament, how did we come to develop such dogma about eternal torment?

Who was the next in line to proclaim burning in Hell?

John the Baptist?

Christ?

Or did someone else have their say before them?

CHAPTER 5:

TOO MANY IRONS IN THE FIRE

'The spider turned her about, and went into her den,

For well she knew the silly fly would soon come back again;

So she wove a subtle web in a little corner sly,

And set her table ready to dine upon the fly...

Alas! alas! How very soon this silly little fly,

Hearing her wily flattering words, came slowly flitting by.

With buzzing wings he hung aloft, then near and nearer drew,

Thinking only of his brilliant eyes, and his green and purple hue-

Thinking only of his crested head- poor foolish thing! At last

Up jumped the cunning spider, and fiercely held him fast.

She dragged him up her winding stair, into her dismal den,

Within her little parlor- but he ne'er came out again!'[24]

How vital is it that we know who it is speaking to us- especially in matters of life and death!

The fly would testify to that if he could!

THE APOCRYPHA

And if we trust the Bible, we're confident in instruction from the likes of Paul and Peter and John, and Christ Himself.

In the same way, those believers twenty and thirty centuries ago were just as sure of their own teachers:

Moses, David, Isaiah, etc... Maybe more so.

In every age, we have believed the inspired scripture.

Always God is faithful to send a steady stream of prophetic voices throughout Israel's history.

Until Malachi's day.

The era from about 400 B.C. to the time of Christ is known as *the Intertestamental Period*, when God did not speak to men, at least not corporately, officially.

They listened in vain nonetheless.

Some ventured to write what they imagined God might be saying as 'the Age of Silence' wore on.

These writings were collected, and entitled the *Apocrypha*, and the *Pseudepigrapha*.

The word *Apocrypha* comes from the medieval Latin *apocryphus*, meaning 'secret' and from the Greek adjective

ἀπόκρυφος (*apocryphos*), meaning 'obscure' or 'hidden'.

Most scholars agree that these extra-biblical books were rightly excluded from the canon (those books determined to have been inspired by the Holy Spirit).

The word *Pseudepigrapha* comes from the Greek ψευδής, *pseude*, 'false' and ἐπιγραφή, *epigraphē*, 'name' or 'inscription'.

Basically, 'false name'.

These books were authored by people who claimed the names of historical figures from the Bible, though we know they weren't.

DID I HEAR YOU RIGHT?

It might be said that because God was not speaking, men volunteered to speak on His behalf.

A contract drawn up by one party without the other's consent is rarely a good thing- how much more when the outcome is the word of men, stamped with divinity?

While much of this Intertestamental *history* is accurate, these bodies of work seemed to take a more harsh and desperate tone with Israel.

1 Ezra 22.10-12 teaches that *'sinners when they die and are buried in the earth and judgment has not been executed on them in their lifetime. Here their spirits shall be set apart in this great pain till the great day of judgement and punishment and torment of those who curse for ever and retribution for their spirits. There He shall bind them for ever.'*[25]

Right off the bat, we can see deviation from the clarity of the quiet *sheol* in the Old Testament (see chapter 1).

More scenarios of *Hell* were painted, animating more of man's touch on eternal matters.

Of the state of the wicked, 1 Enoch 100.9 predicted, *'Woe to you, ye sinners... In blazing flames burning worse than fire shall ye burn.'*[26]

Judith 16.17 says, *'The Lord Almighty will take vengeance on them in the day of judgment; fire and worms he will give to their flesh; they shall weep in pain for ever.'*[27]

Ah, there it is.

Explicit eternal torment- found first here in the words of men thought to speak for God.

It continued elsewhere, as in 4 Maccabees 12.12.

'Justice has laid up for you intense and eternal fire and tortures, and these throughout all time will never let you go.'[28]

AND THROW AWAY THE KEY

Believe it or not, the Book of Jubilee 36.9-11 is even more severe.

'...and he shall depart into eternal execration: so that their condemnation may be always renewed in hate and in execration and in wrath and in torment and in indignation and in plagues and in disease for ever.'[29]

2 Enoch seems to borrow images from Greek myth in 10.1, describing *'a very terrible place, and [there were] all manner of tortures in that place: cruel darkness and unillumined gloom, and there is no light there, but murky fire constantly flaming aloft, and [there is]a fiery river coming forth, and that whole place is everywhere fire, and everywhere [there is] frost and ice, thirst and shivering, while the bonds are very cruel, and the angels fearful and merciless, bearing angry weapons, merciless[ly] torture.'*[30]

We could go on and on, but I think it best to move onto Christ's teaching from here.

Suffice it to say that the Jewish concept of Hell took a hard turn away from the cautious unknown of scripture into sadistic detail not found in the biblical texts.

More than that, they seem to have taken and run with realism many images the biblical writers reserved for apocalyptic *symbolism*, as we saw earlier.

To be fair, there are a number of apocryphal texts that also seem to indicate annihilation, but at this point, that's neither here nor there.

If anything, it proves our point. What we see during this period is *inconsistency*, and overreach past inspired scripture, our only measure of eternal things. [31]

As we're studying the view of Christ at this point, some say *"What about*

Jesus' words, that **'the children of the kingdom shall be cast out into outer darkness: there shall be weeping and gnashing of teeth.'** Mt 8.12

"Isn't this a clear statement of eternal torment in Hell?"

LOSERS, WEEPERS AND GNASHERS OF TEETH

Jesus actually spoke of **'weeping and gnashing of teeth'** on a few occasions.[32]

Let's take a look back at scripture to see if there's any precedent here.

This phrase is seen six other times.

Five of those occasions describe not the tormented, but actually the *tormentor*.[33]

The exception is found in Psalm 112.

Of the ten verses of this psalm, the first *nine* portray how the righteous man lives.

At last, the final verse reads, **'The wicked shall see it** [the righteous man's life]**, and be grieved; he shall gnash with his teeth, and melt away: the desire of the wicked shall perish.'**   Ps 112.10

Like the other five references above, the wicked man is faced with the honor of the godly man - **'he shall see it, and be grieved'**.

In misery and bitter envy, the wicked looks on to see that the godly **'shall not be moved for ever: the righteous shall be in *everlasting* remembrance.'**   v.6

This is likely a snapshot of the Final Judgment, where the wicked can only gnash his teeth in rage and remorse as his own life does slip away, or more specifically **'melt away'** (v.10).

Again, this is language not of torment, but of nonbeing.

And what about the **'weeping'**?

We've all heard the offhanded bravado, *'Yeah, when I get up there, I'm gonna give God a piece of my mind- he's gonna hear it!'*

Guillebaud remarks, 'The instinct, which so often makes even the suicide struggle desperately for life at the last, will surely be far more powerful as the soul faces the final disintegration of personality, the utter end, and what an awful end! How terrible the process of destruction will be will depend on the degree of each soul's guilt before God.'[34]

This makes sense.

WHO WANTS TO GO TO FIRE LAKE?

'Men fear death,' wrote Francis Bacon, *'as children fear to go in the dark; and as that natural fear in children is increased with tales, so is the other.'*[35]

Will justice be meted out according to the sin each man brought to the grave?

While the mild rebel who politely refused salvation may suffer just a blink of Hellfire before he ceases to exist, is it not a fair inference that the unrepentant rapist and murderer of children will likely stay in that fire as long as God's perfect judgment requires?

Imagine the real horror of people who refused to ever come out from the dark.

They now stand before the Lord Jesus Christ, in blinding glory that dwarfs the sun.

They are wakened from the graves, naked on the floor of Judgment. No place to hide any longer.

Eyes of those who scoffed and denied Him behold the dreadful majestic splendor of God.

They're dying to go to Him, and at the same time, too terrified to do it. Hearts implode with despair as they are washed in the holy beauty of the Lamb but cannot go to Him.

Eternal realization hits.

Immediately they know- all of their hollow days had ached with a hidden pain.

Nights when they cried out *'Meaningless!'* are understood in an instant. The Meaning sits before them.

He is the One they blindly longed for without knowing it.

His face is sad and grave, and begins to fade like a mirage.

Slowly, a vast terrible gravity begins to swallow them backward into the yawning chasm.

They feel the life drawn out of their being, as they are drawn away from Life Himself.

Helplessly, they watch the healing beauty of God disappear.

I have no doubt that the lost will weep and gnash their teeth in bitter regret when they awaken to find that they will live no longer.

Certainly **'weeping and gnashing of teeth'** illustrate extraordinary desperation, but any clear detail of its *duration* is simply not there.

Eternity has been read into these verses, plain and simple.

SETTING THE WORLD ON FIRE

*'But isn't this **'weeping and gnashing of teeth'** caused by Hellfire?'*

Let's look at the effect of the fire that raged in Isaiah 42:

**'So He poured out on him the heat of His anger
And the fierceness of battle;
And it set him aflame all around,
Yet he did not recognize *it*;
And it burned him, but he paid no attention.'**   v. 25

Evidently, this fire was **'poured out on'** the disobedient in **'the heat of His anger'**.

But they *'never knew what was happening'* (GNT).

Israel was **'set on fire round about'** and **'it burned him'**, but **'he paid no attention'** (NASB).

How can people broiling in a fire of God's judgment not know it?

If this is God's warning of Hellfire, they will know it according to the doctrine of Eternal Conscious Torment. The victim's consciousness is explicitly stated.

Is it possible that Western scholars have read Hellfire into Middle Eastern texts that describe the fire of a pagan military invasion?

After all, this fire is also described as **'the fierceness of *battle*'**.

The **'weeping and gnashing of teeth'**, **'the worm that dieth not'**, **'the fire that is not quenched'** are common longstanding examples of *Jewish apocalyptic symbolism*, warning of military conquest by pagan nations.

A FURNACE OF FIRE

To be clear, what I am not saying:

I have not said that these passages are already fulfilled in history, and play no future role.

They certainly will.

What I am saying:

There is just no solid evidence to support that the **'unquenchable fire'** of Mark 9 must indicate *eternal* Hellfire, or that sinners will burn forever in it.

In point of fact, scriptural precedent weighs in favor of prophetic symbolism that defines either an appointed judgment in the earth or an undefined period of limited time in **'the lake of fire'** (Re 20.15).

"But Jesus says they are **'cast into a furnace of fire'***; this must refer to eternal Hell!"*

Nowhere is this defined, or even implied as being eternal.

We're reminded by Middle Eastern scholars that our perspective in the West is far removed traditionally and culturally from that of the Jews by thousands of years, and the historical overhaul of men centuries after this.

CHAPTER 6

BOW TO THE KING

During the eleventh century, Canute the first Danish king of England took the throne.

Legend has it that he was a clear spoken man who had grown wary of the many lackeys in his court who tirelessly fawned and flattered.

Their simplest response might be embellished with, *"Certainly, Your highness, there is nothing you cannot do"*, or *"Of course, you are the great Monarch of all. Nothing dare disobey you!"*

One morning the king was walking the shore at dawn under an orange sky with some of his courtiers as they planned the defense of the region.

Once again, a simple *Yes* inflated into *"Absolutely, Your majesty. None can withstand your word."*

In pensive thought, the king stopped for a moment.

He turned to a pair of lads, "Fetch me a chair, please."

"A... a *chair*, your highness?"

"Yes- a chair. At once."

As the lads hurried off, the king turned to the men of his court, dismayed, looking to one another cautiously, "So, you say I am the greatest man in the world?"

A gusty round of affirmation came immediately.

Canute's prime minister took a step forward, "The world bows before you, and gives you honor."

"I see," he motioned to the lads to set the chair down on the wet sand, "Closer to the water."

He sat, and looked out at the ocean, "The tide is coming in. Will it stop if I give the command?"

An uncomfortable dismay settled over the company of men, but none of them had the courage to counter his odd statement.

The prime minister spoke with hesitation, "Give the order, O great king. It will obey."

"Very well," the king turned to the ocean, and bellowed at the waters, "Ocean- I command you to come no further! Waves- stop your rolling! *Do not touch me!*"

In the awkward silence, the surf could be heard pounding in. Seawater and foam drenched his feet.

"How dare you!" the king shouted, "Ocean, turn back now! I have ordered you to retreat before me! And now you must obey me!"

The king seemed to rest in the waves that rushed forward to soak his ankles and cloak.

The men of his court said nothing, half of them wondering if he was mad, and half of them beginning to understand this stark object lesson.

The king turned to survey the ashen faces of these men, "It seems I do not have quite so much power as you would have me believe. Perhaps you have learned something today. Perhaps now you will remember that there is only one King who is all-powerful, and it is He who commands the seas, and holds the oceans in the hollow of His hand. Reserve your praises for Him."

Many of the royal officers hung their heads in open shame, and it's said that soon after, Canute would no longer wear the royal crown as a reminder of that lesson.

RUNNIN' WITH THE DEVIL

Canute's own King also had hard words for some in His court.

Of course, any examination of Christ's view of Hell would be incomplete without *Matthew 25*.

'Then He will also say to those on the left hand, 'Depart from Me, you cursed, into the everlasting fire prepared for the devil and his angels:

for I was hungry and you gave Me no food; I was thirsty and you gave Me no drink;

I was a stranger and you did not take Me in, naked and you did not clothe Me, sick and in prison and you did not visit Me.

"Then they also will answer Him, saying, 'Lord, when did we see You hungry or thirsty or a stranger or naked or sick or in prison, and did not minister to You?'

Then He will answer them, saying, 'Assuredly, I say to you, inasmuch as you did not do *it* to one of the least of these, you did not do *it* to Me.'

And these will go away into everlasting punishment, but the righteous into eternal life.'   Mt 25.41-46

A couple of things we notice.

It may be noted, *'Yes, and that eternal punishment is known as 'eternal judgment' (He 6.2), and 'eternal destruction'!*   2 Th 1.9

We're reminded that the adjective **'eternal'** can be understood to describe its effect rather than its duration.

Eternal punishment is not likely eternal torment.

How so?

Destruction that goes on forever doesn't qualify as destruction, because destruction *never actually takes place*.

Throughout the never-ending process, the subject is never actually destroyed.

By the same token, *judgment* that goes on forever doesn't qualify as judgment.

Throughout the never-ending process, the subject is never actually judged.

There's another bombshell dropped on us in Chapter 8, when we look closer at this in our section on Paul's teaching.

So- is it reasonable to equate this punishment as being the very judgment we see elsewhere in scripture?

If these all describe one and the same event- the aftermath of the Judgment Seat of Christ- yes, it stands to reason.

If the judgment and destruction are final, is it possible that this *punishment* is also final?

I think so.

A LITTLE PIECE OF HEAVEN

Someone asks, fairly:

'If Hell isn't eternal in this passage, then Heaven can't be eternal either! You can't have it both ways.'

A good observation.

Right there in the final verse of Matthew 25, we see **'everlasting punishment'** and **'eternal life'**- *aiOnian kolasin* and *aiOnion zoe*.

Yep- the same word describing each state.

Because we carefully handle the Greek *aiOnion* in detail later, I shamelessly kick that can down the road to Chapter 13.

For now, the JVL reminds us plainly that, even today, 'Regarding the hereafter, Jewish teachings on the afterlife are sparse: the Torah, the most important Jewish text, has no clear reference to afterlife at all.'[36]

Virtually all Jews tended to read the text as cautiously describing an indefinite period of time which may or may not be eternal.

More often we see in the Prophets visions of a people several hundred years old living in peace, prosperity and superhealth.[37]

They seem to announce a new dawn of mankind, like those who lived for centuries before the Flood of Genesis 7.

On his tour of Paradise, John sees Trees of Life bearing the fruit of Life, to be eaten every month. Hebrews living under the shadow of the Roman Empire might have seen here the invitation to a sort of super long afterlife free in a richly blessed earth.

But not necessarily eternal.

WHO'S A GOOD BOY?

'And these will go away into everlasting punishment'

Today's preacher often reads this text aloud, closes his Bible and begins to summon images of lost people pulled into Hell.

But traditional interpretation of the passage seems to overlook the actual qualifiers Christ mentions in this passage, service to the **'hungry or thirsty or a stranger or naked or sick or in prison.'**

If this text outlines the terms by which we all enter Paradise or the Lake of Fire, how do you think you're doing?

Honestly.

How is it looking for you as you run down the to-do list of verses 41-43?

Who among us can say we check off each of the six good deeds here on a regular basis?

If I'm honest, I'd start walking to the goat section as soon as I got up there, and save Him the trouble of telling me.

And as personal merit goes, as long as we're being real honest, I imagine I'd be waving goodbye forever to some *'unsaved'* people I know, as they rightfully take their place in the sheep section!

We can meditate on this text. We can let it move our hearts for the less fortunate. And find an outlet to serve them.

But I believe it would be a mistake to base our eternal destinies on our performance of these.

It can't be denied that there are parabolic elements of this text, but to what degree they weigh into the nature of its literal meaning is debatable.

Also, discussion around the Greek word for *punishment* should give us pause.

It's notable that the word Christ used for **'punishment'** is the word *kolasin*.

KOLASIN

As the goats are culled from the sheep, they face **'everlasting punishment'**- *aiOnion kolasin*.

Now here's a mind-bender.

Its root *kolasis* was also used in ancient Greek literature.

Josephus used this word to recount... the death penalty.

Also, in the apocryphal books of the day, such as 2 Maccabees 4.38, 'Then Antiochus had this bloodthirsty murderer put to *death*. This was how the Lord gave him the punishment he deserved.'

Again, the contemporary use of the word for 'death sentence' is- *kolasis*.

While these are not inspired scripture, they show us how the word was commonly used at that time. If anything, *kolasis* often meant *execution*.

Even more intriguing is the discussion around the Greek word for eternal- *aiOnios*.

What if the word **'eternal'** here doesn't actually *mean* eternal, as we understand it?

The most literally correct translation of *aiOnios* is not **'eternal'**, but **'age-lasting'** or **'age-enduring'**, as rendered by Young's Literal Translation and the Concordant Version.

What's the difference?

And why the literal nitpicking with such versions?

AiOnios is the adjectival form of *aion*, meaning 'age', 'season' or 'eon'.

In classical Greek, *aiOnios* is used to describe very long periods of time, such as the reign of the Caesars, or the length of a war.

But of course, these men and wars don't still continue today.

We'll give this matter of *aiOnios* more thorough study in Chapter 13.

For anyone wanting to know more on this subject, Appendix 1 is recommended reading.

In the meantime, some of you are reminding me that Christ had more to say about Hell than this. Let's go there.

We can leave no stone unturned.

CHAPTER 7:

NOT A CHANCE IN HELL

In an age when superstition often had a tighter hold on human hearts, men like Christopher Columbus were warned not to set sail for the Indies.

He was chastised that his vessel and crew would plunge over the edge of the earth and fall into Hell itself.

Who appointed this airheaded careless fellow as an admiral over any decent ship?

Did he not recognize the deep scarlet hue at sunset on a given evening?

Nightfall as red as this was thought to be the end of an uncommonly bloody day on that side of the world, perhaps a war, for it was said to be the reflection of a myriad of souls dying and sliding into the underworld to burn forever.

While few men in fifteenth century Europe had anything good to say of him, Columbus' name was also mentioned from time to time- in the lectures of one Nicolaus Copernicus.

As a youth, Copernicus was intensely interested in physics and mathematics; by age twenty-one, he was the prodigy of the University of Cracow, and was soon invited to teach mathematics in Italy.

But his raging passion became... astronomy.

By the calculus of the sky and geometry of the earth, Copernicus insisted: no one is going to fall off the face of the earth, just as giant angels had no role in moving the sun behind the hills at night, or rehanging the stars each evening like Christmas tree ornaments.

In polite defiance of the great Ptolemy, Copernicus dared to proclaim that the universe wasn't actually revolving around the earth; *The Almagest* had been ironclad scientific law for fourteen centuries.

Who was this pompous twenty-one year old buffoon trying to 'dethrone God by a yardstick'?

Priests and bishops publicly scolded him.

He was tagged with the label 'heretic' by low and high men alike.

But it wasn't until a cardinal from the Vatican came to call that

Copernicus was halted.

He was cautioned, 'Why stir up trouble for us, speaking things unauthorized by His Majesty the Pope? Wouldn't the Lord be better served by keeping the peace?'

Being a man of honor, Copernicus withdrew to Poland, where he took the position of a country clergyman in the quiet village of Frauenburg, forbidden by Rome to speak on 'volatile issues'.

And yet, his soul couldn't help but stare and ache at the array of infinite stars glimmering night after night, whispering, demanding his attention.

By day he faithfully visited the flock, and kept the parish register.

By night, he gazed out the huge skylight he had cut out of the old farmhouse roof, where he studied.

Each and every night for twenty-seven years, he watched the heavens, fine-tuned his primitive instruments, recorded his findings.

Of the stars, he said, 'They do me great honor. I am forbidden to converse with great men, but God has ordered for me a procession.'

'Surely God will not damn me for wanting to know the truth about his glorious works,' Copernicus declared, 'To look at the sky and behold the wondrous works of God, must make a man bow his head and heart in silence. I have thought, and studied, and worked for years, and I know so little.'[38]

A full forty years finally saw the completion of his book *On the Revolutions*, but to send it to Rome for permission to publish was not an option.

He couldn't risk either its rejection, or destruction.

Finally, on his deathbed, Copernicus ventured to send his life's work to

Pope Paul III, whom he felt may look past the epithet 'heretic', and allow its publication.

On May 24, 1543, a messenger from Nurembourg arrived at the bedside of the fever-stricken Copernicus.

In his hands was placed a nicely bound copy of the decades-long manuscript prayed and labored over for most of his life.

It is said that he held it to his old, weary chest, closed his eyes one final time and exhaled his last breath in seventy years.

Thank God for men like Copernicus. If he had been too afraid of the opinions of his peers and overseers, he would never have forged ahead with the science men after him found so valuable.

Like Jesus, he was something of an iconoclast.

He simply would not yield to soften the facts.

Even in a culture stacked so heavily against him, he could not compromise plain truth to appease those who were uncomfortable with it.

HELL AND TRUTH

The New England Primer warned early pioneers:

> *Time cuts down all,*
>
> *Both great and small.*
>
> *While youth do cheer*
>
> *Death may be near.*

If we're going to be looking at these mentions of Hell by Christ, we'd better examine Luke 16.19-31, arguably the main proof text of proponents of Eternal Torment.

Luke 16.19-31:

'Now there was a rich man, and he habitually dressed in purple and fine linen, joyously living in splendor every day.

And a poor man named Lazarus was laid at his gate, covered with sores,

and longing to be fed with the *crumbs* which were falling from the rich man's table; besides, even the dogs were coming and licking his sores.

Now the poor man died and was carried away by the angels to Abraham's bosom; and the rich man also died and was buried.

In Hades ['hell'- KJV] he lifted up his eyes, being in torment, and saw Abraham far away and Lazarus in his bosom.

And he cried out and said, 'Father Abraham, have mercy on me, and send Lazarus so that he may dip the tip of his finger in water and cool off my tongue, for I am in agony in this flame.'

But Abraham said, 'Child, remember that during your life you received your good things, and likewise Lazarus bad things; but now he is being comforted here, and you are in agony.

And besides all this, between us and you there is a great chasm fixed, so that those who wish to come over from here to you will not be able, and *that* none may cross over from there to us.'

And he said, 'Then I beg you, father, that you send him to my father's house—

for I have five brothers—in order that he may warn them, so that they will not also come to this place of torment.'

But Abraham said, 'They have Moses and the Prophets; let them hear them.'

But he said, 'No, father Abraham, but if someone goes to them from the dead, they will repent!'

But he said to him, 'If they do not listen to Moses and the Prophets, they will not be persuaded even if someone rises from the dead"'.

At first glance, this does appear to be a divine testimony of Hell.

Many preachers believe they take their cue from Christ when preaching Eternal Torment from this passage.

Closer inspection may be warranted.

From a cultural perspective, it's important to keep in mind that we are reading a parable spoken by a 1st century Jew *to* 1st century Jews.

A parable is a story with symbolic meaning.

I've heard teachers affirm that this was definitely not a parable.

How do they come to this conclusion?

It follows six consecutive parables, all involving stewardship.

Its tone is that of storytelling, **'There was a certain rich man...'** exactly like the parable immediately before it in Luke 16.1, **'There was a certain rich man...'**

As Jesus often bundled parables together in clusters for emphasis (see the parables of the lost coin, lost sheep, and lost son in Luke 15, for example), so he aligns these.

And as he was speaking in public here (v.14), we're reminded that **'All these things Jesus spoke to the crowds in parables, and he *did not speak to them without a parable.'*** Mt 13.34

ABRAHAM WAS

Also, this matter of the rich man being awake in torment, and Abraham and Lazarus consciously awaiting **'the resurrection at the last day'** (Jn 11.24), we have investigated thoroughly in Chapter 1.

Scripture indicates that they were likely **'them which are asleep'**.[39]

Someone may argue, *'But Jesus said that Abraham rejoiced to see his day, and was glad. That means Abraham was alive to have seen Jesus' ministry.'*

A fair point.

Let's peek at that text.

'Your father Abraham rejoiced to see My day, and he saw *it* and was glad."

So the Jews said to Him, "You are not yet fifty years old, and have You seen Abraham?"

Jesus said to them, "Truly, truly, I say to you, before Abraham was born, I am."' Jn 8.56-58

Essentially, Jesus may have been stating to the rulers, 'When I say Abraham rejoiced to see my day, you assume I describe your day. But I pre existed Abraham. I lived before Abraham walked the earth around

1800 B.C. I revealed myself to him *then*'.

It's intriguing that Christ does not say that Abraham *is*, but that he *was*.

The evidence seems to say that Abraham may sleep in *sheol,* as all men.

Surely Abraham rejoiced at the visitations in Genesis 15, 18, etc..., when he was alive on the earth many centuries before Christ was born in flesh.

We also see obvious emblems in the parable which, again, would have rung like a bell to those ancient Jewish hearers, among which is a rich man **'clothed in purple and fine linen'**, a token of nobility and royalty.

And then we notice the feature of a beggar **'desiring to be fed with the crumbs which fell from the rich man's table'**.

What are we reminded of here?

Remember the Syrophenician woman who sought the blessing of God for her daughter, demon-possessed?

When this Gentile was told this was reserved for the Jews only, **'she said, Truth, Lord: yet the dogs eat of the crumbs which fall from their masters' table.'** Mt 15.27

Her plea was heard, though Gentiles were loosely called everything from heathen to beggar to dog to infidel, etc...

And the symbolism emerges yet more.

BEGGARS CAN BE CHOOSERS

Now consider the fact that the beggar is named, while the rich man is not.

Rather than awakening to the throne of God, they both go to meet Abraham at their death.

No one else seems to be there.

This is plainly an anomaly of **'the resurrection at the last day'**.

Abraham seems to *know* this man Lazarus.

Astonishingly, this all comes into even clearer focus when we recognize that Lazarus is the Greek translation of the Hebrew *Eliezer!*

See Genesis 15.2, **'And Abram said, Lord GOD, what will you give me, seeing I go childless, and the steward of my house is this Eliezer of Damascus?'**

This Gentile servant of the patriarch was his *steward*, of all things. The metaphor is strikingly plain in a parable of stewardship.

Whether they were tax collectors, harlots, beggars, those from east, west, north & south, or even simply *stones*, Christ hammered this point time and again.

Wards of the natural line of Abraham weren't necessarily entitled to anything.

Gentiles (and Hebrews) who trusted Christ were (Mt 3.9; 21.31; Lk 13.29; etc...).

The rich man could plead with Abraham as **'Father'**, **'father'**, **'father...'** (vv. 24,27,30) as long as he liked, a constant appeal of the Jews.

But it wouldn't change the fact that this believing Gentile was on his way to **'the resurrection of the just.'**   Lk 14.14

ABRAHAM'S BOSOM

The term **'Abraham's bosom'** may sound strange to us in our time and time zone.

The word found in the Greek text for **'bosom'** is *kolpos*, meaning 'lap'.

This describes the eastern practice of reclining at one's dinner table with guests, the closest of whom was said to lie on the *bosom* or chest of the host (see Jn 13.23).

We're reminded that before Ishmael or Issac were born, *Eliezer* was Abraham's adopted son, who stood to inherit his wealth and surely reclined on his right at the table.

To Jews made to memorize the Torah from childhood, this was self-evident.

Unmistakably, this is a *parable*, and its players patently symbolic of Jews and Gentiles, the fates of which would depend upon their response to Christ.

So how did this cultural divide we are looking across now get *so* wide?

CHAPTER 8:

DEAD MEN TELL NO TALES

There's the old story of the gate into Hell.

One poor fellow faced the Pearly Gates a moment after his death only to find St. Peter standing there with an icy scowl.

The apostle pointed to the left, in the direction of a nasty little corridor, plunging away into the dark.

The fellow slumped away, and made his way into the awful tunnel.

Inside, he observed two more dingy little passageways, one marked *'Men'* and the other *'Women'*.

With a sigh, he shuffled ahead into the Men's entrance to discover yet two more archways.

The first was inscribed: 'Men Who Were Dominated by their Wives'.

That line of sad souls was horrendously long indeed.

The sign above the other gate read 'Men Who Dominated their Wives'.

The fellow straggled over to a lone scrawny lout in front of that doorway, and asked him why he had to wait there.

'I don't know. My wife just told me to stand here.'

Again, they're little anecdotes like these that creep into our thoughts of Hell over time, as a society.

OK. Can you think of a greater heavyweight than the apostle Paul when it comes to understanding of the afterlife?

Did he think of Hell like we do?

Francis Chan, who leans heavily in the direction of eternal torment, concedes 'the first thing to notice is that he never used the word. Did you get that? Paul *never* in all of his thirteen letters used the word *hell*.'[40]

A good point.

Thankfully, we can also read Paul himself.

In all of Paul's recorded public preaching, the only occasion where he might be seen as remotely touching on Hell is found in Acts 17.

'Therefore having overlooked the times of ignorance, God is now declaring to men that all *people* everywhere should repent,

[31] because He has fixed a day in which He will judge the world in

THE SLUMS of HEAVEN

**righteousness through a Man whom He has appointed, having
furnished proof to all men by raising Him from the dead'**   vv. 30-31

We see judgment here- surely none of us disagree with that.

But *Hell*, specifically eternal conscious torment, we just do not find.

DEAD AS A DOORNAIL

If eternal torment in Hellfire was the inevitable fate awaiting most of
humanity, Paul spoke precious little of it in his speeches archived in
Acts, and in his fourteen books of scripture *(or just 13, if he didn't
author Hebrews)*.

In fact, he never mentioned it.

If eternal torment is an established doctrine of the Church, I'm afraid we
have to conclude that Paul fumbled this badly.

Is that a fair assessment?

**'Therefore I testify to you this day that I am innocent of the blood of
all men** [27] **For I have not shunned to declare to you *the whole counsel
of God.'***   Ac 20.26-27

**'[T]hrough mighty signs and wonders, by the power of the Spirit of
God; so that from Jerusalem, and round about unto Illyricum, I have
fully preached the gospel of Christ.'**   Ro 15.19

Let's take a closer look at what Paul himself has assured us is **'the *whole*
counsel of God'**, **'fully preached'**.

Romans 1.32, 'who knowing the judgment of God, that they which commit such things are worthy of **death**, not only do the same, but have pleasure in them that do them.

Romans 2.12, 'For as many as have sinned without law shall also **perish** without law: and as many as have sinned in the law shall be judged by the law;

Romans 6.16, 'sin unto **death**'

Romans 6.21, 'the end of those things is **death**'

Romans 6.23, 'For the wages of sin is **death**'

Romans 8.13, 'if ye live after the flesh, ye shall **die**'

1 Corinthians 1.18, 'the preaching of the cross is to them that **perish** foolishness'

1 Corinthians 15.22, 'in Adam all **die**'

2 Corinthians 2.15,16, 'For we are unto God a sweet savour of Christ, in them that are saved, and in them that **perish**'

2 Corinthians 3.7, 'for the letter **kills**'

Galatians 6.8, 'Whoever sows to please their flesh, from the flesh will reap **destruction**'

Phillipians 1.28, ' This is a sign to them that they will be **destroyed**'

Phillipians 3.19, 'Their destiny is **destruction**'

2 Thessalonians 1.9, 'who shall be punished with everlasting **destruction** from the presence of the Lord, and from the glory of his power'

2 Thessalonians 2.10, 'with all deceivableness of unrighteousness in them that **perish**'

Hebrews 6.8, 'that which bears thorns and briers *is* rejected, and *is* nigh unto cursing; whose end *is* to be **burned**'

Hebrews 9.14, 'cleanse our consciences from acts that lead to **death**'

Hebrews 10.27, 'a fearful expectation of judgment and of raging fire that will **consume** the enemies of God'

THE SLUMS of HEAVEN

Hebrews 10.39, 'we do not belong to those who shrink back and are **destroyed'**

THE *OLETHRON*

We see here lots of warning of judgment and death.

But eternal torment we do not find.

At this point, someone may say, *"Whoa! We can't just blow by 2 Thessalonians 1.9! That says 'everlasting destruction'!"*

It does- rather than everlasting *torment, burning, pain,* etc.., consistent with all of the references listed above.

Death and *destruction* explicitly convey the *end* of a thing rather than a continual course of action.

Again, if this process of destruction were eternal, its objects would *never actually be destroyed*.

Destruction would never take place, a principle we touched on in Chapter 6.

More than that, we see the word for **'destruction'** here is *olethron*, literally rendered *extermination*, or *whole ruin!*

TWO 'DESTRUCTIONS'

Some may argue that the phrase **'everlasting destruction'** is redundant in the event that this destruction is final.

I have to disagree.

Because there are *two* deaths, **'everlasting destruction'** is perfectly accurate.

Every person has, or will experience the first death [temporary destruction], and will be laid to rest (Ge 3.19).

Whether it be quickly or over time, he will experience decay.

Yet this is not *everlasting* destruction, because every one of us will raised up on the Last Day, **'for the hour is coming, in the which *all* that are in the graves shall hear his voice,**

and shall come forth; they that have done good, unto the resurrection of life; and they that have done evil, unto the resurrection of damnation.' Jn 5.28-29

At that time, those who have rejected Christ will experience **'the second death'**.[41]

This will be the destruction that is final and everlasting.

Also, we can't ignore the strange phrasing at the end of the verse, when the damned **'shall be punished with everlasting destruction from the presence of the Lord, and *from the glory of his power.'*** 2 Th 1.7-9

Somehow, the **'glory of his power'** appears to play a role in the destruction of the wicked.

It calls to mind that fire that fell from heaven in Leviticus.

After Moses and Aaron had prepared the sacrifice, **'the glory of the Lord appeared unto all the people. [24] And there came a fire out from before the Lord, and consumed upon the altar the burnt offering and the fat: which when all the people saw, they shouted, and fell on their faces.'** Lv 9.23-24

Just two verses later, Aaron's drunken godless sons make a mockery of the tabernacle, and **'there went out fire from the Lord, and devoured them, and they died before the Lord.'** Lv 10.2

This sacred fire that consumed the offering was the same that **'devoured'** the wicked.

Now let's peek in at what the rest of the New Testament writers have to say.

THE MOUTH OF TWO OR THREE WITNESSES

It seems the apostle James agreed, **'There is *only* one Lawgiver and Judge, the One who is able to save and to destroy.'**   Ja 4.12

Like Jesus in Matthew 10.28, James is clear.

There are two ultimate destinies for men- to be saved or *destroyed*, not saved or endlessly tormented.

And he's not done.

He reiterates, **'What is your life... You are just a vapor that appears for a little while and then *vanishes away.'***   Ja 4.14

An equally important metaphor is found in Jude.

'Even as Sodom and Gomorrah, and the cities about them in like manner, giving themselves over to fornication, and going after strange flesh, are set forth for an example, suffering the vengeance of eternal fire.'   Jd 7

Again, this sounds like the fire that **'is not quenched.'**   Mk 9.44

Is the literal fire that fell on the region of Sodom still raging in the desert today? Of course not.

As we've seen, this implies judgment- the duration of which is not addressed.

Without question, **'eternal'** in this passage describes the **'vengeance'**, not a literal fire.

Any other inference is conjecture, unless we're willing to violate rules of basic sentence construction.

'Hey! That's from Peter's epistle, isn't it?' someone remarks.

Pretty darn close.

Peter also covered this topic, **'And turning the cities of Sodom and Gomorrah into ashes condemned them with an overthrow, making them an example unto those that after should live ungodly.'** 2 Pt 2.6

The RSV has here, **'condemned them to extinction'**.

The phrase **'turning... to ashes'** means just that. Thayer's lexicon has 'reduce to ashes'.

But before we can close this section on the New Testament, the apostle John reminds us he wrote a little epilogue called *The Revelation*.

CHAPTER 9:

REVELATION IN THE REVELATION

Just this past week, a recent video was brought to my attention.

A little crudely put together, I was surprised to see well over 2 million views, and thousands of *'likes'*.

What was it they liked?

A young lady from Ecuador claims to have been escorted by the Lord on four occasions (so far) to experience Hell- and to warn humanity of what she saw.

There, she insists that she watched blood-bought Christians roasting in Hellfire, gnawed by worms and bound by snakes. What sin brought them to the horrid place she describes?

A wide range of crimes had sealed their fates.

Such as?

She saw worship leaders who played 'the wrong kind' of music in Church, burning for their error.

She watched rebellious children in the flames. They had played video games and watched 'bad' programs on TV.

Other sins?

Not giving enough money to the Church.

Suicide.

Unfulfilled ministry callings.

Listening to secular music.

If we're to accept this testimony at face value, it would appear to plunge the Church into a strange cryptic legalism. Does this square with the Word of God?

And does this sound like the *heart* of God?

"But she saw literal people crawling in literal fire and worms! This is a lot like what the Apostle John saw!"

Is it?

While I won't comment on the validity of her story, I'll just say that she's young and may not fully understand what she claims to have seen, in terms of historic symbolism.

How so?

For instance, in the book of Revelation John saw a beast and a great prostitute also burning in the Lake of Fire. Is this literal?

No. There won't be a literal beast thrown into the Lake of Fire.

Why not?

Because this beast is a symbol.

This **'beast'** is largely understood by scholars to represent the pagan Roman Empire (Da 7.7-8,23; Re 13.1-7), collapsing against the force of Odoacer's surge, leading the Heruli barbarians into Rome.

They took it in A.D. 476.

THE GREAT PROSTITUTE

What about the great prostitute?

'And again they shouted: "Hallelujah! The smoke from her goes up forever and ever."'   Re 19.3

Is this literal?

No. How do we know this?

Because the great prostitute is defined in Revelation 17.18, **'The woman who you saw is that great city, which reigns over the kings of the earth'**.

She is a city- a world system.

So we see that, just as there won't be literal **'goats'** (Matthew 25) or **'trees that do not bear good fruit'** (Matthew 3) burning, neither will there be a literal beast, or a giant hooker burning.

These are symbols with a deeper meaning.

I believe John would point out to devotees of this young lady that his own vision was **'signified'** (Re 1.1) to him- given to him in *signs* and *symbols*.

BACKGROUND CHECK

Speaking of John – he had a few more things to say about the final judgment.

Some of you have been on the lookout for this passage through this entire book.

Well, here it is:

'And the third angel followed them, saying with a loud voice, If any man worship the beast and his image, and receive his mark in his forehead, or in his hand,

The same shall drink of the wine of the wrath of God, which is poured out without mixture into the cup of his indignation; and he shall be tormented with fire and brimstone in the presence of the holy angels, and in the presence of the Lamb:

And the smoke of their torment ascends up forever and ever: and they have no rest day nor night, who worship the beast and his image, and whosoever receives the mark of his name.' Re 14.9-11

Again, from the very first verse of the Revelation, John asserts that the vision was **'signified'** to him- shown to him in emblems that signify events yet to come.

As we ought to be careful with the way we handle symbols like **'a beast rising up out of the sea, having seven heads and ten horns'** or **'locusts like unto horses... [with] faces of men. And... the hair of women, and.. the teeth of lions.. and tails like unto scorpions'**, so should we avoid running headlong with this passage.

Here we read that **'the smoke of their torment ascends up forever'**.

SMOKE- BUT NO SMOKING GUN

Consider Psalm 37.20:

'But the wicked shall perish... into smoke they shall vanish away.'

It is *their smoke* that ascends up, not their cries, torture, etc...

There before **'him who is able to destroy both soul and body in hell'**, the wicked will **'vanish away.'**

Professor Oral Edmond Collins comments, 'Clearly, the language is used to describe temporal punishment, everlasting in effect not in process. The figure of smoke rising "forever and ever" is used to indicate the permanence of the destruction... [and] indicates a permanent memorial'.[42]

Also, this prostitute is addressed as Babylon, **'the great city, which reigns over the kings of the earth.'** Re 17.18

As classic apocalyptic literature, The Revelation shares the same symbolism as earlier apocalyptic.

Notice especially the companion text of Isaiah 34.9,10:

'And the streams of Edom shall be turned into pitch,
  and her soil into brimstone;
  her land shall become burning pitch.
Night and day it shall not be quenched;
  its smoke shall go up for ever.
From generation to generation it shall lie waste;

  none shall pass through it for ever and ever'.

If Isaiah were to finish the chapter here, could we be persuaded that volcanoes erupted all over Edom, and that the lava still burns to this day?

We know nothing like that has happened.

We have just read that the land will become burning sulfur, fire and magma that will *never* go out.

And yet in the following verses, we are told that *after* this, the land is inhabited by owls, hedgehogs, ravens, jackals, tree snakes and *pelicans*, of all things!

Impossible, if this were literal in any sense.

This is simply imagery for a city overthrown and deserted.

How so?

In the 6th century B.C., nomadic Arab tribes decimated Edom.

Every human being was slaughtered or driven out. Animals came to feast on the corpses and infested these ruins for decades.

After Edom's conquest, literal fire did not continue to burn there forever, but *the judgment itself* was final.

ECHOES OF ISAIAH

Let's keep in mind the metaphors used by the Holy Spirit in each of these fascinating companion texts.

Isaiah: **'her soil [shall be turned into] into brimstone'**

Revelation: **'he shall be tormented with fire and brimstone'**

Isaiah: **'its smoke shall go up for ever'**

Revelation: **'the smoke... goes up for ever'**

Isaiah: **'night and day it shall not be quenched'**

Revelation: **'there is no rest day nor night'**

Each of these passages are prophetic symbolism, and each warn of the imminent end of those who ignore God's word.

It may be pointed out that the phrase **'night and day'** some claim as an indicator of literal endless time.

We should be reminded that Paul wrote that he was **'laboring night and day'** and **'night and day praying exceedingly that we might see your face'**.[43]

We understand not to read these with wooden literalism where it is not intended.

YOUNG SPEAKS

Lastly, Robert Young of *Young's Literal Translation* and *Young's Analytical Concordance* rightly reminds us of the heavier emphasis on the *present* tense of the Greek *proskuneo*, that **'they have no rest day and night, who *are bowing before* the beast and his image.'**

Re 14.11 YLT

Notice it is *while* they are on the earth, bowing before the beast (who, like them, will be dealt with at time's end) that they have no rest.

Also keep in mind that, at this point, we are nowhere close to the end of all things.

There are eight full chapters of the book of Revelation yet to occur.

Speaking of which, let's dare to look into those dark episodes.

THE FALSE FALSE PROPHET

'And the beast was seized, and with him the false prophet who performed the signs in his presence, by which he deceived those who had received the mark of the beast and those who worshiped his image; these two were thrown alive into the lake of fire which burns with brimstone.

And the rest were killed with the sword which came from the mouth of Him who sat on the horse, and all the birds were filled with their flesh.' Re 19.20-21

Again, let's reiterate.

The Revelation is apocalyptic symbolism.

The beast and the false prophet (the beast with **'horns like a lamb'**- Re 13.11) are symbolic.

Of what?

We're reminded that this beast **'ascends from the bottomless pit'** (Re 11.7).

That's not likely a human being.

Like the great prostitute, the beast and the false prophet are metaphors and not people.

"But what about 'the false prophet'? *Prophets are people!"*

ARE THEY ALWAYS?

We actually see **'the false prophet'** referred to as **'another beast'**.[44]

Neither Satan nor the beast is a human being.

And here the false prophet is grouped together with them in Revelation 16.13.

The likelihood that this describes a man when the others do not is slim.

Of these beasts, Edward William Fudge concludes, 'They are not actual people but representations of persecuting civil government and corrupting false religion. Neither institution will be perpetuated forever, nor could either suffer conscious, sensible pain... The language is symbolic and a literal interpretation is impossible. Political power and apostate religious beguilement are not persons who can be tortured in fire. Even the vision would be impossible if these forces were not personified as creatures.'[45]

DOWN IN FLAMES

Finally, John scrawls the *very last word* on Hell.

'And death and hell were cast into the lake of fire. This is the second death.' Re 20.14

It's never mentioned again.

Remember how we promised to touch on the difference between *Hell* and the Lake of Fire?

Someone says, *"But Hell is the Lake of Fire!"*

Evidently not.

Like a rat eaten by a dog, Hell is 'eaten' by the Lake of Fire.

Though the two may look alike, the one is undeniably distinct from the other.

And like the rat, Hell is swallowed up.

WHOSOEVER NOT WRITTEN IN THE BOOK OF LIFE

Shockingly, **'hell'** appears to meet *its final end*- along with death and **'whosoever was not found written in the book of life.'** 20.15

And just a few verses later, John hears a voice from heaven declaring **'there shall be no more death, neither sorrow, nor crying, neither shall there be any more pain: for the former things are passed away.'**   21.4

Interesting! That would seem to preclude any weeping and burning in Hellfire.

This makes sense.

Revelation 20 closes with the end of Hell.

Revelation 21 opens with the end of weeping and suffering.

'But,' someone will say, *'the early church must have kept our doctrine pure!'*

Some did.

But over the centuries, imperfect men strayed from God's clear path.

And some forged new paths for those who knew no better than to follow.

Now- onto the second century.

CHAPTER 10:

PAVED WITH GOOD INTENTIONS

"See on the middle of that red-hot floor stands a girl: she looks about sixteen years old. Her feet are bare. Listen; she speaks. "I have been standing on this red-hot floor for years! Look at my burnt and bleeding feet! Let me go off this burning floor for one moment!"

'The fifth dungeon is the red-hot oven. The little child is in the red-hot oven. Hear how it screams to come out; see how it turns and twists itself about in the fire. It beats its head against the roof of the oven. It stamps its little feet on the floor.

'*God was very good* to this little child. Very likely God saw how it would get worse and worse, and would never repent, and so it would have to be punished more severely in hell. So God in His mercy called it out of the world in early childhood".[46]

In J. Furniss' old Catholic tract (1882), we are shown an awful graphic picture of Hell.

Or is it?

I have to say. I don't recall reading of red-hot ovens or 'the fifth dungeon' anywhere in scripture.

As we have moved through both the Old and New Testaments (and those centuries between them), we have now fine tuned our views to the word of God, where men have carelessly blurred them.

Just how did Mr. Furniss and other likeminded preachers come to these notions?

Enter the second century.

BLURRED LINES

The philosophers Athenagorus (A.D. 127-190) and Tertullian (A.D. 160-220) were among the first converts to Christianity to weave the philosopher Plato in with Paul.

Among their conclusions:

Because Plato asserts that the human soul has no end, the equation is settled.

Everyone who goes into the Lake of Fire must either:

1) come through it to be taken up into heaven, or

2) burn forever.

Tertullian admitted as he crafted his teaching, "I may use, therefore, the opinion of a Plato when he declares, 'Every soul is immortal.'" (Tertullian, 3)

His capitulation to Greek philosophy posed a problem he failed to see.

Of the six major schools of theology in the first several centuries of the Church, there was only *one* that initiated teaching the doctrine of eternal torment- that of *Carthage, North Africa.*

And guess who the star pupil of this institution was?

None other than *Tertullian,* Carthage-born (A.D. 160-220), and a lucid writer, orator, lawyer and theologian.

At this same time, those of the Coptic, Syriac, Armenian, Greek and Ethiopic schools chose to carefully maintain the integrity of the Greek Septuagint and *Textus Receptus.*

But the school of Carthage had largely moved on from the Greek texts and relied more heavily on Latin copies.

And where Tertullian began to blossom in his theories of eternal Hellfire, Augustine (A.D. 354-430) grew broad and ample branches out of this view.

'By far the main person responsible for making hell eternal in the Western Church was St. Augustine. Augustine was made bishop of Hippo in North Africa. He did not know Greek, had tried to study it, but stated that he hated it... it is his misunderstanding of Greek that cemented the concept of eternal hell in the Western Church... So complete was his concept of God's exclusion of non-Christians that he considered un-baptized babies as damned. When these babies died, Augustine softened slightly to declare that they would be sent to the 'upper level' of hell. Augustine is also the inventor of the concept... known as *Purgatory.*'[47]

'Augustine, who later outdid Tertullian and his doctrines, maintained that the whole human race was "one damned batch and mass of perdition" (conspersis damnata, massa perditionis), out of which a few are elected to salvation, while all the remainder are lost forever.'[48]

GAME-CHANGER

In sports, one team will often break through with a play so decisive and unstoppable that the game seems hopelessly out of reach for the other team.

Commentators sometimes call this a *game changer*.

Scholar Alexander Thomson relates one major game changer that took place in the debate over eternal torment in the 6th century.

'[W]e shall cite one more similar yet very instructive case. The Emperor Justinian was the greatest of the Eastern (Byzantine) Emperors. He reigned from 527 to 565 at Constantinople. In the year 534 he published in fifty volumes the world famous "Justinian Code" of Laws. This was a digest of the Greek and Roman constitutions, ordinances, and legal decisions, culled from two thousand manuscript volumes, and it forms the basis of most medieval and modern codes of law. In the year 540, Justinian made arrangements for the calling together of the famous local council of four years later. He was determined that certain doctrines must be suppressed.

'In setting forth the position when writing to the Patriarch Mennas of Constantinople, he discussed the doctrines with great ability. In particular, he wished it made very plain that the life of the saints was to be everlasting, and that the doom of the lost was to be likewise.

'*Yet he did not argue that the word eonian meant everlasting. Nor did he claim that the word eonian had hitherto been misunderstood.*

'But writing in the very expressive Greek language, Justinian says, "The holy church of Christ teaches an *endless eonian* (*ateleuteetos αιωνιος*) life for the just, and *endless* (*ateleuteetos*) punishment for the wicked." *Justinian knew quite well that by itself* eonian *did not signify endless, and he therefore added a word the meaning of which is quite unequivocal, a word not found in the Scriptures.*

'This letter of Justinian, which is still in existence, ought to convince anyone who is in doubt, regarding the true scriptural meaning of this word *eonian*.'[49](emphasis mine).

Emperor Justinian, more a ruthless political man than a theologian, recognized the benefit of Eternal Torment as a leveraging tool to motivate the masses to comply.

As the Roman System assumed greater and greater influence over Carthage, they were expected to closely follow suit.

They did.

OBJECTION, YOUR HONOR!

And yet there were many who did not see eternal torture in the texts.

Augustine himself admitted, '[I]ndeed *very many*... do not believe that such things [eternal torment] will be' (Enchiridion, 112- emphasis mine).[50]

Of the four General Church Councils held in the first four centuries: *Ephesus, Nicea, Constantinople* and *Chalcedon*, none asserted the position of eternal Hellfire.

None.

In fact, the Niceo-Constantinopolitan creed adopted in A.D. 325 by 320 bishops, says only one thing about the future world:

'Christ will come again to judge the living and the dead.'[51]

There is no mention of eternal torment.

And yet it seemed clear to them that every immortal soul, **'not found written in the book of life was cast into the lake of fire.'**   Re 20.15

Those who (rightly) could not teach eternal torment, as it was not established in scripture, had to think long and hard about this dilemma of the immortal wicked.

If they *are* to live forever, then there must be a way out of that nasty place!

119

SWEET CLEMENTINE

Along came *Clement* of Alexandria (A.D. 150-213), highly educated in classical Greek philosophy and literature, especially Plato and the Stoics.

He determined to 'set himself... to make a summary of Christian knowledge up to his time', and penned *Miscellanies*.[52]

Arguably the most influential scholar of the second century, he rejected the concept of eternal torment, alleging 'some he converts by penalties, others who follow him of their own will, and in accordance with the worthiness of his honor, that every knee may be bent to him of celestial, terrestrial and infernal things (Phil. 2:10), that is angels, men, and souls who before his advent migrated from this mortal life... But God does not punish (*timoria*), for punishment is retaliation for evil' (*Stromata*, VI, ii., Pedag. 1,8; on 1 John ii.,2).[53]

HELL HATH NO FURY

One of Clement's pupils was a man by the name of Origen.

He also learned at the feet of one Ammonius Saccas, a teacher of Neoplatonism and its underpinning of the immortal soul.

Origen was the first to write a complete systematic theological commentary of the entire Bible, and he who took up the gauntlet against pagan philosopher Celsus, who put forth a scathing work called *The True Word*- an attack of the Christian faith.

Origen's reply was entitled simply *Against Celsus*.

It seems that Origen's kind heart could not figure an equation involving immortality, and the Lake of Fire.

The inevitable result- godless immortal souls cannot, and therefore *will not* die in the Lake of Fire.

So when met with passages such as Romans 9, where God was cited as hating Esau, Origen went on to add a pinch of the far east.

He attributed this sad fate to the failure of Esau, and other rebels in previous lives.

Those disembodied souls who sinned the worst were flung back into earth as demons, while those who sinned the least were made angels.

Folks 'in the middle' would continue to reincarnate on their way toward perfect piety.

In fact, Origen is notorious for having taught that *Satan* could even be saved after successive cycles in the earth!

For this statement (among others), the Second Council of Constantinople (A.D. 553) rightly castigated him, albeit a couple hundred years after his death.[54]

GREGORY TOES THE LINE

Not long after, Gregory (A.D. 335-394) bishop of Nyssa in Cappadocia took part in the Council of Nicea and later Councils.

In *Orat. Catech.*, Gregory continued Origen's line of thinking.

'When all the alloy of evil that has been mixed up in the things that are, having been separated by the refining action of the cleansing fire, everything that was created by God shall have become such as it was in the beginning...'[55]

The edicts declared by the Seventh General Council of A.D. 787 reveal the doctrinal schizophrenia of the era.

Among them:

1) All assembled agreed that Gregory of Nyssa be granted one of the highest medieval titles given to men, "Father of Fathers"'.

2) And yet, through the political pressure of men like Justinian, this same Council *declared a curse* upon all those who taught that the fire of

God be defined as anything other than the instrument of eternal torment.

They had celebrated the very heretic they had condemned in the same day! [56]

We see now the dilemma of the Greek philosophers in the Church.

Plato taught that the soul is always immortal.

Therefore, a wicked immortal soul either *had to* escape hellfire, or *had to* burn forever, often depending on one's personal sensibilities.

It was an impasse.

Any other option was unthinkable.

And the dogma set in deeply over the centuries, so much so that burning human beings alive at the stake became routine.

It was not uncommon for the Inquisitors, or Queen 'Bloody' Mary herself to shrug off pangs of guilt with replies such as, 'I only do here on earth what my God will continue to do to them perpetually.'[57]

PAPER TRAIL

It isn't well known that a number of later prominent patrons of eternal torment weren't quite as set in stone as we have been told.

Many Traditionalists gave a hearing to the great works of Conditionalists Constable, Froom, Petavel and others.

While Jonathon Edwards preached on the perils of refusing an Angry God, he said very little in opposition to Conditionalism.

In an essay entitled *Concerning the Endless Punishment of Those Who Die Impenitent*, he fires a barrage of about 15,000 words at Universalism broadside.

But no more than *three sentences* does he volley in the direction of Conditionalism, and concedes, 'it answers the scripture expressions as well, to suppose that they shall be annihilated immediately, without any long pains, provided the annihilation be everlasting.'[58]

In his book *The World to Come*, Issac Watts was as rigid a champion of eternal torment as any.

But by the time he wrote *The Ruine and Recovery of Mankind*, he was willing to ask if final judgment might not include 'the utter destruction of the life of the soul as well as of the body', that God may in fact 'utterly destroy and annihilate His creatures for ever'.[59]

Charles Spurgeon, along in years stated, 'I have no quarrel with the Conditional Immortality doctrine'.[60]

PARADISE LOST IN THE SHUFFLE

Even John Milton (1608-1674), author of the classic *Paradise Lost*, made it clear that he wrote as a poet, rather than a theologian.

As a measure of correcting the mania of readers having taken his book and run with it, he offered the question 'that he who had sinned in his whole person, should die in his whole person?'

For instance, in that very work, he offered,

'... It was but breath

Of life that sinned; what dies but what had life

And sin? The body properly had neither.

All of me then shall die: let this appease

The doubt, since human reach no further knows.'[61]

With a doctrine unlike many Baptists today, the General Baptist Elders of 1660 presented Charles II with *A Brief Confession or Declaration of Faith*.

While Article 21 asserted the resurrection of both the just *and* the wicked, Article 22 followed up to affirm their utter extinction:

"The triumphing of the wicked is short, and the joy of the Hypocrite but for a moment; though his excellency mount up to the Heavens, and his head reach unto the clouds, yet shall hee perish for ever, like his own dung; they which have seen him shall say, Where is hee?"[62]

Others such as Issac Newton, Samuel Clarke, and William Whiston came to this same conclusion.

GUILT BY ASSOCIATION

Some may press the claim that Conditionalism is cursed, as it was picked up by strains of the Jehovahs' Witnesses and the Seventh Day Adventists.

This is true. It was.

Be that as it may, this is also irrelevant.

Those who reject Conditionalism because a cult may happen to have adopted it do a disservice to themselves and to logic itself.

This is a common logical fallacy known as the *Hypothetical Proposition*.

A *Hypothetical Proposition* states that if A is false, then B must also be false.

Therefore, if the Seventh Day Adventists are a cult, therefore Conditionalism must be untrue.

Point taken.

I disagree with a number of SDA views.

Immediately though, one finds they are then stuck with the fact that the SDA also hold many orthodox views as well: salvation in the shed blood of Christ, the Virgin Birth, the Second Coming of Christ, etc...

Are we willing to refuse those doctrines, too?

If not, Conditionalism, like any other doctrine, must stand or fall alone by scripture and history, regardless of who does or doesn't believe it.

CHAPTER 11:

THE BURNING QUESTION

A smug professor stood before his freshman class, chalk in hand.

All these fresh faces, held in suspense. The first day of the semester was always such a good opportunity to knock their socks off with some cheeky sacrilege.

He seemed to derive so much pleasure from the gasps and raised eyebrows as he opened with something like:

"There is no 'god' in heaven," he began, *"If any god exists, we have already met them in the most educated people among us."*

They looked stunned, uncomfortable.

With a smirk, the professor turned briskly on his heel.

The chalk clicked and clacked as he attacked the blackboard with broad strokes.

God is other people, it read.

The professor loved to preside over this awkward silence, and slowly scan the room.

"Sir?" a young lady strode to the front, and gestured for the chalk, "May I?"

Mildly amused and curious, the instructor forfeited the chalk to her, and watched as she approached the blackboard.

One tiny stroke, and she returned to her seat amid great applause.

The board now read:

God is other, people.

TO BEAT HELL

Whether it be the placement of a comma, a word or the *meaning* of a word, we saw how men were spurred on to see the Church sanction their own views.

Though it took five centuries to gain broad acceptance, Church teaching was tarnished by far more than punctuation.

Upon the foundation of sacred writ were now being laid in bricks of Greek thought, and most notably- the tenet of the *immortal soul*.

Is every soul immortal?

Is every soul eternal?

Might it be fair to search the ancient writers to see what they believed?

How have we developed our views on eternal life over the centuries?

HOW DARE YOU

Am I saying that *no* soul is given immortality?

I am not.

Am I denying the existence of Hell?

If you've read this far, you know very well I'm not.

Traditionalists air sermons with titles such as:

Why I Believe in Hell

Hell is Real!

Yes, I believe in Hell with you.

But its dimensions and duration are debatable.

It may be disputed, *"But God can give everyone eternal life- He can do anything!"*

ADDING FUEL TO THE FIRE

This is true.

Edward William Fudge answers this point well.

He writes, 'The issue really becomes a matter of exegesis. Since God is *able* to preserve or to destroy His human creature, what does scripture *indicate* that He *will* do to those He finally expels to hell?'[63]

As we've covered, Hell is a very certain reality.

But we've also seen how the Church has at times largely depended more on tradition and presumption, than rigorous study of scripture as to what Hell *actually is.*

While I expect to get plenty of pushback here, I also expect those who may disagree to walk through scripture with me and investigate this concept of the immortality of the soul.

Traditional?

Without a doubt.

But is it scriptural?

From the age-old Epic of Gilgamesh to the Bhagavad-Gita to the tales of Ponce de Leon in his quest for unending life in a fountain to today's obsession with beauty, all cry the same thing:

'I want to live!'

And how long will that be?

Most of us would check *No expiration date*.

Something in every human being would like to live forever, because God **'has also set eternity in their heart.'**   Ec 3.11

Why?

As beings made in the image of God, were we created with *potential* immortality?

Is there a destiny that has ached in our spirit for thousands of years back to Genesis?

ON ONE CONDITION

'And the LORD God commanded the man, saying, Of every tree of the garden you may freely eat.

But of the tree of the knowledge of good and evil, you shall not eat of it: for in the day that you eat of it, you shall surely die.'   Ge 2.16-17

At this point, Adam and Eve were permitted to eat from the tree of life.

Whether they did or didn't, we do not know.

But it appears to have been open to them.

'Of *every* tree of the garden you may freely eat'.

That would have included the Tree of Life.

How long they may have eaten from it and lived we do not know.

The *only* tree they were forbidden was... *The Tree of the Knowledge of Good and Evil.*

As we know, they tasted it.

Talk about food poisoning!

'Then the Lord said, "Now that the man has become as we are, knowing good from bad, what if he eats the fruit of the Tree of Life

and lives forever?"

So the Lord God banished him forever from the Garden of Eden, and sent him out to farm the ground from which he had been taken.

Thus God expelled him, and placed mighty angels at the east of the Garden of Eden, with a flaming sword to guard the entrance to the Tree of Life.' Ge 3.22-24

This is conditional immortality.

Now in our fallen nature, none of us can push through a clearing into Eden, and snag a piece of fruit from the tree of life, to cheat death and judgment.

It will not happen.

No man, nor army of men will ambush the throne of God, and seize the promise of eternal life. He is 'the King of kings, and Lord of lords, who *alone* has immortality.' 1 Ti 6.15

OFF LIMITS

Basically, if God is OK with human beings in eternal corruption (resembling our popular concept of Hell), He might have just let Adam and Eve go ahead and help themselves to the tree of life after 'sin entered into the world.' Ro 5.12

But He did not.

More than that, Genesis teaches that Adam 'begat a son in his *own* likeness, after *his* image.' 5.3

A corrupt mortal man fathered corrupt mortal sons- from whom *we* have come.

God **'ALONE has immortality'**.

'But the Bible says man became "a living soul"!'

True.

However, the identical Hebrew words are translated as **'living creature'** describing common animals in Genesis 2.19 and 9.12.

Will every mouse and mosquito, earwig and frog be granted eternal life?

Maybe.

'But the Bible says we have eternal life!' some will point out.

Again, true- for those of us who have come to **'our Savior Jesus Christ, *who* has abolished death and brought life and immortality to light through the gospel.'**   2 Ti 1.10

How is immortality given?

'Through *the gospel'*.

At this point, some may object on the grounds that **'God said, Let us make man in our image, after our likeness'** (Ge 1.26), *therefore we all must have eternal life too!'*

If this reasoning were true, why would we stop at immortality?

Couldn't we all then expect other divine attributes like omniscience, omnipotence and omnipresence for ourselves as well?

ORDERS STRAIGHT FROM THE TOP

Comedian Steven Wright says dryly, *'I intend to live forever. So far, so good.'*

Christ Himself actually defined this question in the clearest terms.

'Jesus said, "Truly I say to you, there is no one who has left house or brothers or sisters or mother or father or children or farms, for My sake and for the gospel's sake,

but that he will receive a hundred times as much now in the present age, houses and brothers and sisters and mothers and children and farms, along with persecutions; and *in the age to come*, eternal life.'

Mk 10.29-30

Notice that this promise of eternal life is spoken only to those who sacrifice **'for the gospel's sake'**.

Remember how the scribes sent men **'to catch him in his words'**?

Mk 12.13

One of those episodes unfolded like this.

'Now there came to Him some of the Sadducees (who say that there is no resurrection),

and they questioned Him, saying, "Teacher, Moses wrote for us that IF A MAN'S BROTHER DIES, having a wife, AND HE IS CHILDLESS, HIS BROTHER SHOULD MARRY THE WIFE AND RAISE UP CHILDREN TO HIS BROTHER.

Now there were seven brothers; and the first took a wife and died childless;

and the second and the third married her; and in the same way all

seven died, leaving no children.

Finally the woman died also.

In the resurrection therefore, which one's wife will she be? For all seven had married her."

Jesus said to them, "The sons of this age marry and are given in marriage,

but those who are considered worthy to attain to that age and the resurrection from the dead, neither marry nor are given in marriage;

for they cannot even die anymore, because they are like angels, and are sons of God, being sons of the resurrection.'   Lk 20.27-36 NASB

This seems indisputable.

Only **'those who are considered worthy to attain to that age** (*aion*) **and the resurrection from the dead'** are they who **'cannot... die anymore, because they are like angels'**.

It seems that the lives of those who are *not* considered worthy to attain... end.

WHO WANTS TO LIVE FOREVER?

We see there are two ages spoken of here: **'this age'** and **'that age'**.

'*This* age' Jesus referred to life in the fallen earth, where **'they did eat, they drank, they married wives, they were given in marriage.'** Lk 17.27

Or, as we are sometimes heard to say, 'On *this* side of heaven'.

And **'this present evil age'** (Ga 1.4) is driven largely by **'the god of this**

age.'   2 Co 4.4; 1 Jn 5.19; Re 12.9

This age.

'*That* age' he has defined in context- **'the resurrection from the dead'**.

So **'this age'** is the time before the resurrection of the dead, and **'that age'**, that which comes after.[64]

Plain enough.

But Jesus has said something staggering here.

There are, of course, many who will *not* attain to **'that age'**.[65]

They are not found worthy to come into **'that age'**, and will die **'the second death'** (Re 2.11; 20.6,14; 21.8), which is **'everlasting destruction.'**   2 Th 1.9

They are *not* made like the angels.

It appears they will not live forever.

How so?

FIRE PREPARED FOR THE DEVIL AND HIS ANGELS

'Since, then, the children have a common physical nature as human beings, he also became a human being, so that by going through death as a man he might destroy him who had the power of death, that is, the devil;

and might also set free those who lived their whole lives a prey to the fear of death. It is plain that for this purpose he did not become an angel;

he became a man, in actual fact a descendant of Abraham.'

                        He 2.14-16 PNT

Simply, Christ is God.

God cannot die.

Angels cannot die.

Men can die.

Christ came to die for men.

Therefore, **'for this purpose he did not become an angel; he became a man.'**

This is why Christ revealed that there is a place of **'everlasting fire, prepared for the devil and his angels.'**   Mt 25.41

If they live forever, they may be kept there forever.

He does not say 'prepared for the devil and his angels, *and wicked people'*.

EVERY MAN A PHEONIX?

Peter put it this way, '**for you have been born again not of seed *which is perishable* but imperishable, that is, through the living and enduring word of God.'**   1 Pt 1.23

Peter is so very clear.

He is teaching those who '**have been born *again*'**.

He describes not our first birth by '**seed which is... perishable'** [human birth, which must end in death], but our *second* birth by '**seed which is... imperishable'** [can never die].

Any human being who chooses to reject the imperishable seed will not be forced to live forever, as God designed it.

This is exactly what Christ taught in Luke 20.

And as Paul taught the Corinthians:

'But now Christ has been raised from the dead, the first fruits of those who are asleep [not 'burning in torment'].

For since by a man *came* death, by a man also *came* the resurrection of the dead.

For as in Adam all die, so also *in Christ* all will be made alive.

But each in his own order: Christ the first fruits, after that those who are Christ's at His coming.' 1 Co 15.20-23 NASB

Who will be made alive?

'Those who are Christ's'.

WHO WILL BE MADE ALIVE?

Hear Jesus' words in John 5.

'Truly, truly, I say to you, an hour is coming and now is, when the dead will hear the voice of the Son of God, and those who hear will live.

For just as the Father has life in Himself, even so He gave to the Son also to have life in Himself;

and He gave Him authority to execute judgment, because He is the Son of Man.

Do not marvel at this; for an hour is coming, in which all who are in the tombs will hear His voice,

and will come forth; those who did the good deeds to a resurrection of life, those who committed the evil deeds to a resurrection of judgment.' Jn 5.25-29

Here the objection may be raised, *'Yes, and that judgment is known as eternal judgment in Hebrews chapter 6!'*

Agreed.

ETERNAL REDEMPTION

Again, judgment that lingers endlessly does not qualify as judgment, because judgment is never finally rendered.

When a Judge bangs the gavel down, he has judged.

The man convicted is then removed from the courtroom to carry out his sentence.

The judge is not the bailiff, nor the warden, nor the prison guard, etc...

He has judged. Judgment is complete.

The sentence carried out afterward is a different thing altogether.

Consider Hebrews 9.12, **'Neither by the blood of goats and calves, but by his own blood he entered in once into the holy place, having obtained eternal redemption for us'**.

'eternal redemption'?

Are we being endlessly redeemed?

Our redemption is not a process that continues forever, never quite finished.

In fact, **'It is finished'** and it is eternal.   Ps 19.30

Its result stands forever.

The judgment we see carried out in the book of Revelation is perfectly consistent with Genesis.

TAKING THE LONG VIEW

God designed this in perfect balance.

He would not allow men to live forever crippled and haunted by sin.

That would be a monstrous curse, a long cruel bottomless descent into mental and physical agony as sin mastered and ruined every one of us.

In Noah's time, **'God saw that the wickedness of man was great in the earth, and that every imagination of the thoughts of his heart was only evil continually.'** Ge 6.5

If men aged just *hundred*s of years plunged the old world into chaos, imagine the bloodbath and pain of the eternal victims of eternal wicked men.

And yet God would not sentence men to trudge the earth as flesh automatons, either.

A heartless clone cannot really live, and love.

Man could not be programmed to love.

So man would be entrusted with this beautiful, vulnerable treasure of life with free will.

But... not so fast.

Eternal life is altogether different.

Man was offered immortality on one condition.

Man violated that one condition. Immortality was withheld.

Until when?

Until Jesus **'brought life and immortality to light through the gospel'**.

Think of the plain meaning this gives to Jesus' words, **'Truly, truly, I say to you, if anyone keeps My word he will never see death.'** Jn 8.51

There was a monumental day when the apostle John peered into the sky from a grassy hilltop outside Bethany, watching Jesus ascend up into the clouds.

As an old man decades later, he was visited and heard these words from the mouth of the risen Christ, **'him who overcomes will I give *to eat of the tree of life,* which is in the midst of the paradise of God.'**   Re 2.7

The way to the tree of life is now opened.

God's wisdom is astonishing.

MISINFORMATION CAMPAIGN

Have you ever heard a politician stand up and just openly lie to his constituency?

And yet, his rival usually follows an unwritten political law.

Rather than call their opponent a 'liar', they generally stay with terms such as 'less than honest', 'stretching the truth', 'short on integrity', etc...

'Liar' is so blunt and impolite and... accurate.

We Christians tend to observe a similar unspoken rule.

Rare is the plain-spoken 'eternal torment' or 'burning in hell forever' that would seem to convey the plain truth with matter-of-fact clarity.

We usually opt for the softer 'separation from God', or 'shut outside the gates', or 'missed heaven'.

While all these may be true, why do we avoid the crucially serious details of that 'separation' by not speaking in the most honest and candid terms?

If there was ever a man who said exactly what He meant, and meant exactly what He said, it was Christ.

What words did He use?

CHAPTER 12:

THE REASON HE CALLS IT

'THE LAST DAY'

An old Jewish folktale tells of two brothers brought up in the heart of the city.

Never having seen field or farm, they were a little confused upon their first journey to the countryside.

"What's he doing?" one brother pointed out off the dirt road, to a farmer behind his workhorse, guiding the big iron plow through the meadow, "He's ruining the grass!"

THE SLUMS of HEAVEN

On the way back, again the brother scowled, as they watched the farmer sowing wheat into the furrows, "This fool is mad. What kind of imbecile throws away perfectly good grain right in the dirt like that? I cannot stand to be around this idiocy any longer! I'm going back to the city where people have some sense!"

But the other brother found a place beneath the shade of an old tree, to watch the farmer work.

Every few days, he would stroll by, and after a few weeks, he understood.

He wrote his brother, recounting how the neat rows of lush green shoots turned to tall golden sheaves standing up from the earth.

As it happens, the city brother came by during harvest.

Scythe in hand, the farmer began to hew the crop down with wide swaths of his sickle.

The city boy turned with a withering stare to his brother, "Now look what you've done! You summon me all the way out here just to watch this lunatic hacking his own plants down with a weapon! Have you also lost your mind? Why don't you go out and ruin his plants with him then, you half-witted clod!"

With that, he returned to the city for good.

The patient brother, on the other hand, observed as the farmer carefully collected the wheat to the granary, and separated the chaff, to be left with fat bags of rich wheat.

"This is how it is with God's works, too," he nodded, "We mortals only see the beginning of His plan. We do not understand the full purpose unless we pay attention, and trust in His wisdom."

WHISTLING PAST THE GRAVEYARD

Augustine points out, 'Where a very serious crime is punished by death and the execution of the sentence takes only a minute, no laws consider that minute the measure of the punishment, but rather the fact that the criminal is forever removed from the community of the living.'[66]

Fast forward to the late nineteenth century.

What comes around goes around. The Apocryphal views of Intertestamental literature had shouldered their way in to find a place in most churches.

Greek scholar and translator of the New Testament R.F. Weymouth pushed back.

'My mind fails to conceive a grosser misinterpretation of language than when the five or six strongest words which the Greek tongue possesses, signifying "destroy" or "destruction", are explained to mean maintaining an everlasting but wretched existence. To translate black as white is nothing to this.'[67]

Of course, this was nothing new.

While there had been men centuries earlier who refused to waste their time listening to Jesus, or even hoped to best him in an intellectual duel, **'the common people heard him gladly.'**   Mk 12.37

Notice how certain Jews framed their questions.

'And, behold, one came and said unto him, Good Master, what good thing shall I do, that I may have eternal life?' (Mt 19.16) and **'Master, what shall I do to inherit eternal life?'**   Lk 10.25

Each of these men had heard Christ preaching.

They did not ask Him, 'Master, what shall I do to inherit eternal life *in heaven,* and *not in hell'*?

They heard Him teach, **'And fear not them which kill the body, but are not able to kill the soul: but rather fear him who is able to destroy both soul and body in hell.'**   Mt 10.28

He did not preach, 'Rather fear Him who is able to *torment forever* both soul and body in hell'.

He taught**, 'He that loves his life shall lose it; and he that hates his life in this world shall keep it unto life eternal.'**   Jn 12.25

He did not preach, 'Unfortunately, he that loves his life will keep it unto *life eternal in the lake of fire'*.

He also stated, **'I am the living bread that came down out of heaven;** *if* **anyone eats of this bread, he will live forever.'**   Jn 6.51

He did not say, 'If anyone eats of this bread, he will live forever in a much *better place* than he who doesn't.'

Jesus did not misspeak. One appears to live forever and the other does not.

IMMORTALITY

The apostle Paul corroborates, **'to those who by perseverance in doing good seek for glory and honor and immortality, eternal life;**

but to those who are selfishly ambitious and do not obey the truth, but obey unrighteousness, wrath and indignation.

There will be **tribulation and distress for every soul of man who does evil, of the Jew first and also of the Greek.'**   Ro 2.7-9

Notice that those who seek immortality (*aphtharsia*) will be granted eternal life (*aiOnios zoe*).

They are used interchangeably.

Those who are **'selfish and reject what is right'** (GNT) will find trouble and distress, wrath and indignation. But eternal torment is not listed here.

As grave a penalty as that could be, wouldn't we expect Paul to have been faithful to warn us?

WRATH AND MERCY

Someone may point out, *"But it says **'wrath and anger'** there. That may be eternal Hell!"*

Unlikely.

In point of fact, most every biblical example of wrath ends in finality.

Ezekiel writes, **'So I will pour out my wrath on them and *consume* them with my fiery anger, bringing down on their own heads all they have done, declares the Sovereign LORD.'"**   22.31

Psalm 21.8-9 reads, **'Your hand will lay hold on all your enemies;
    your right hand will seize your foes.**

**When you appear for battle,
    you will *burn them up* as in a blazing furnace.
The LORD will *swallow them up* in his wrath,
    and his fire will *consume* them'.**

It's difficult to see eternal torment in these verses.

They seem to state the very opposite- destruction.

A SUDDEN END

Zephaniah also heard some crazy interesting words from heaven.

'Neither their silver nor their gold
   will be able to save them
   on the day of the LORD's wrath."

In the fire of his jealousy
   the whole earth will be consumed,
for he will make *a sudden end*
   of all who live on the earth.'   1.18

Of the Day of the Lord, Zephaniah prophesies **'that day will be a day of wrath— a day of distress and anguish, a day of trouble and ruin.'**

Zp 1.15

There's all that distress and anguish and wrath Paul also warned about.

But for whom?

For **'all who *live on the earth'*.**

He does not warn of an *eternity* of wrath, but **'a *day* of wrath'**.

We are not told that He will sentence them to eternal torture, but that **'he will make *a sudden end'*** of them.

Now let's look at the following passages carefully.

NOT LONG FOR THIS WORLD

The Psalmist writes, **'For yet a little while, and the wicked shall not be: yea, thou shalt diligently consider his place, and it shall not be.'** 37.10

The wicked will have no place after the Judgment. They will no longer exist.

Obadiah recorded, **'All the nations will drink continually. They will drink and swallow and become as if they had *never existed.'*** Ob 16

Isaiah wrote that God's enemies **'will be as nothing and *non-existent.'***

Is 41.12

Again hear the Psalmist **'when the wicked sprouted up like grass and all who did iniquity flourished, it was only that they might be *destroyed forevermore.'*** Ps 92.7

Someone will counter, *"These all seem very conclusive. But they only refer to this mortal life on earth, and not the hereafter."*

A fair point.

Let's consider another similar text.

Solomon wrote, **'there will be *no future* for the evil man; The lamp of the wicked will be *put out.'*** Pr 24.20

Again, it may be argued that this simply means that the evil man's life ends on earth- before he goes to an eternity of torture.

Yet Solomon went on to very clearly qualify this statement when he wrote, **'the spirit of man is the lamp of the LORD, searching all the innermost parts of his being.'**   Pr 20.27

We notice. It is **'the *spirit* of man'** (and not his body) that is his **'lamp'**.

Again, **'there will be *no future* for the evil man'**.

It looks as if his spirit isn't necessarily destined to rekindle to an afterlife of torment.

For the man who defies God, that lamp is **'put out'**.

His very *essence*, his *spirit*, **'the innermost parts of his being'** is brought to an end.

This agrees with Malachi that the wicked will be left **'neither root nor branch'** (Mal 4.1) and with Peter, that the wicked are **'condemned... to extinction.'**   2 Pt 2.6

YOU'RE FIRED- *LITERALLY!*

Do you recall the story Jesus told of the nobleman who went into a far country to receive a Kingdom?

In summary, the nobleman returns to find he must deal with servants who have become his enemies.

We learn something pivotal in this illustration. Did the nobleman send the traitors to the dungeons to be tortured for the rest of their days?

'But those enemies of mine who did not want me to be king over them—bring them here and kill them in front of me.'" Lk 19.11-27

Clearly, the nobleman is an emblem of Christ.

We notice that the **'enemies of mine who did not want me to be king over them'** are executed, and not tortured; **'kill them in front of me'**.

Among the analogies for judgment given by Christ in Matthew and Luke, none are tortured.[68]

In Luke 12, the offender is **'cut in pieces'**, obviously execution.

And of course, Jesus could have used the metaphor of torture to describe the eternal outcome of the damned.

How do we know this?

Because He *already used* this analogy in Matthew 18- an evident example of the self-torment of the bitter and unforgiving.

' "Then the master called the servant in. 'You wicked servant,' he said, 'I canceled all that debt of yours because you begged me to.

Shouldn't you have had mercy on your fellow servant just as I had on you?'

In anger his master handed him over to the jailers to be tortured, until he should pay back all he owed.

"This is how my heavenly Father will treat each of you unless you forgive your brother or sister from your heart." Mt 18.32-35

But in our text of Luke 19, and throughout Matthew, He did not use the metaphor of torture.

The violators were not tortured.

They were *executed*, which would appear to be the imminent end for the damned at the Judgment Seat of Christ.

CHAPTER 13:

TIME WON'T LET ME

A woman found herself standing outside the wispy white Pearly Gates.

St. Peter strolled out, "Hi there".

"Uh... hello," she stuttered as she looked around, "... This is *heaven*, right?"

"It is," he nodded.

As she started timidly through the immense gates, he held up a gnarled hand, "Just a minute, please."

Wide-eyed, she stammered.

Old Peter's eyes scanned his clipboard, "There's just one small test before entrance will be authorized."

She froze.

"Spell the word 'Love'."

"Really?" she stood mouth agape, "I mean- OK... L- O- V- E. Love."

"Correct. Enter thou into the joy of the Lord."

"*Yes'*" a big sigh and a fist pump, and she was striding for the gates.

"Just one sec, though," Peter checked the clipboard again, "Actually, I'm pulling the long shift, and I kind of need to use the restroom. Could you... just take my spot for a minute? I'll be really quick."

"How... I mean, what do I *do?*"

"If any one comes up, just have them spell a word. If they get it right, they're in."

"I'd be honored," she assured him.

It was peaceful watching the clouds float by, and a couple of angels even soared overhead. A few minutes later, who should appear but the woman's loser husband!

She was aghast, "What are *you* doing up here?!"

The fellow blinked, "I don't really know. I was so drunk when I left your funeral. I think I was in an accident. Did I..." he looked around, *"Is this heaven? Am I in?"*

"Not so fast. Pete says you have to spell a word."

"*Pete?*" his brow creased, "You don't mean *Saint* Peter. Oh, you're *buddies* now?"

She crossed her arms, "Pete says you need to spell a word before you get in."

"Fine. What's the word?"

"Czechoslovakia."

FAMOUS LAST WORDS

All joking aside, some folks have held an equally dismissive view of the afterlife, albeit with a more serious tone.

For instance, Edvard Munch said, "From my rotting body, flowers shall grow and I am in them, and that is eternity".[69]

Some take comfort in Munch's cold simplicity.

Others would disagree with such a casual take on eternal matters.

Yet opinions on this topic fall all over the map.

While the last few chapters looked at Theology, this one will take a quick look at *Dialectology*, or *Etymology*, the study of language and its development.

Specifically, we'll look at the word *eternity*.

Why?

Is this important?

The word **'eternal'** in our Bibles doesn't always mean *eternal*, as we may understand it.

So far, we've looked at instances where eternal things are plain symbolism.

Other instances would seem to call for strict literalism.

Do they?

WORD PLAY

Let me ask a few questions.

What do you think of when I ask you to imagine a *passenger*?

Did you think of someone riding in a car, or on a plane?

Or did you imagine someone *walking*?

Strangely enough, the word's original meaning is *'someone travelling on foot'*!

What do you think of when I tell you a building is being *decimated*?

Did you picture a smoking pile of rubble?

Or did you envision a remodeling project where the area of the building is reduced by exactly ten percent?

If you look closely, you can see its initial definition right in the word itself- to decimate means *'to reduce by one tenth'*.

When your child asks what you think of their artwork or essay, you may hear yourself answering *'Terrific!'*

Little do they know (nor do they need to!) that the word's authentic meaning is *'to cause terror or horror'*.

'Sophisticated'?

Initially, it meant *'unnatural'* or *'contaminated'*.

A number of years ago, one might have been overheard commenting on something good with, 'That's *bad!'* (which still meant 'good', by the way).

Even today, a young person's opinion that your car or your outfit is 'Sick!' is probably not an insult. In most cases, you can just smile and thank them.

Now, if a word's meaning can swing to its exact *opposite usage* in a matter of months, just imagine how badly some of our words can be disfigured over a few *hundred years.*

SAY WHAT?

With this in mind, let's look at a couple of these words.

For me personally, the correct definitions of these words will have no ultimate bearing on my final destiny.

I have entrusted my life and soul to the Lord Jesus Christ.

Whether a word really means this or that won't likely matter to me in the long run.

But for many people, the nature of God is on trial.

It's been said, *'God is a million times worse than Hitler!'*

God has been indicted in courts of human opinion of the only crime worse than mass murder- mass eternal torture, exhibit A being this word **'eternal'**.

Does God create billions of souls to burn in eternal Hellfire without a choice?

What if exhibit A is found to be flimsy or faulty?

Anecdotal evidence is often thrown out, and the case reconsidered.

We'll deal with God's character in the next chapter.

In this one, we'll aim to prove beyond a reasonable doubt that the word **'eternity'** is hardly eternal itself.

LONG TIME COMING

'Eternity' is in fact pretty young, as words go.

Let's examine this word often mistranslated as **'eternal'**.

It's the word *aion*, or *eon*.

An eon is defined as:

e·on
  [ee-*uh* n, **ee**-on]

noun

1. an indefinitely long period of time; age.

2. the largest division of geologic time, comprising two or more eras.
*dictionary.com

Though an eon begins and ends at a given point, it may span centuries.

The similarity is unmistakable.

A*ion*= eon.

Eternity, on the other hand, has been described as the state of timelessness (without time) *or* the endless course of time, without beginning or end.

WORD SEARCH

With that, let's see if you can spot the *eonian* (the adjectival form of *aion*) in the following verses.

See if anything looks a little off to you.

Christ Himself explained in one of the parables, **'the harvest is the close of the age** [aiOnos]**; and the reapers are the angels.'**   Mt 13.39; RSV

Young's Literal Translation puts it this way, **'the harvest is a full end of the age** [aiOnos]**, and the reapers are messengers.'**

So far, so good.

Most of us see no problem with these.

Essentially, these translations seem to agree.

THE SLUMS of HEAVEN

For perspective, let's peek at another text.

For continuity, we'll use the same translations.

In his letter to Titus, Paul describes our faith **'in hope of eternal** [eonian] **life which God, who never lies, promised ages** [eonian] **ago.'**   1.2; RSV

Young's (YLT), **'... upon hope of life age-[en]during** [or 'age-long'- *Beecher*]**, which God, who doth not lie, did promise before times of ages.'**

Hmmm OK. Which is it, RSV?

You've used the same word to describe two infinitely different states.

Are we talking about time, or timelessness?

What did God promise men **'ages ago'**?

And why does Young render a weird phrase here, instead of just using **'eternal'**?

Does it matter?

PICKY, PICKY!

There's a reason why Young translated so precisely.

In the Greek interlinear, we find this same word used by Matthew in 13.39, *aiOnos* (another declension of *aion*), translated as **'age'** or **'world'**, basically *eon*, a limited span of time.

So why is the word *aiOniou*, in its clear root and meaning, being translated in Titus as both **'ages'** and **'eternal'** in the same verse?

Greek is far too specific and consistent in its rules of case to be mangled like this.

It appears that the translators took liberties with this word.

Why?

As with *sheol*, they were faced with a conundrum.

Again, they found themselves forced to pick and choose as they tried to reconcile these words with what they had been taught *must* mean a timeless eternity.

WHEN FOREVER ISN'T

Have you ever wondered about texts like Exodus 12.24?

'And you shall observe this event [Passover] **as an ordinance for you and your children** *for ever'*.

OK. Will the Jews be ritually slaughtering lambs in heaven, after they have all died?

Of course not.

They were to **'observe this event as an ordinance'** for an *age*, until the New Covenant was established, and not for eternity.

Exodus 21.6, **'Then his master shall bring him unto the judges; he shall also bring him to the door, or unto the door post; and his master shall bore his ear through with an awl; and he shall serve him for ever'**.

Really?

Will this guy be serving his boss *endlessly, even in heaven or hell*?

What if they don't go to the *same place?!*

Those who insist that phrases such as **'eternity'** or **'forever'** must always be understood as *eternal* in their literal sense may not have given much thought to these verses.

We've all heard someone say, 'I've been waiting *forever!*', when they've usually been looking out the window for about ten minutes!

NIV has instead, '**...pierce his ear with an awl. Then he will be his servant for life.'** Ex 21.6

I'm sure that version sits a little better with us- and with logic and the Hebrew text.

At about this point in the chapter, we're heading into deeper linguistic waters.

If you're unconvinced, or just want to come along for the ride, we're glad to have you.

But if you feel you have the gist of it, we can always meet at our next point- Chapter 14.

LIMITED ETERNITY?

By the way- the Hebrew word used in both of these is *olam (Strong's #5956)*, the exact word the Greek text translates as *aion*- eon, or age.

It means 'beyond the horizon' or 'to conceal'.

Each is designated as a long indefinite period of time.

Other examples of *olam* are clearly temporary.[70]

If you take the time to reference these, it becomes undeniably plain that the words **'eternal'** and **'forever'** are not always to be translated literally.

Also the Old Syriac, very close to the Hebrew, is understood to have been copied from the original Greek texts around the close of the 1st century.

They render the Greek *aion* AND *kosmos* (world) as… *olm*, meaning 'obscure'.

Sound familiar?

This is almost identical to the Hebrew *olam*, and again defines the passing eon, without question.

'Well… there must be some Hebrew word for 'literally endless' in the Bible!'

There is.

ASTRONOMICAL!

For instance, Psalm 147.5 tells us that **'Great is our Lord, and mighty in power; His understanding is *infinite'*.**

We all know what 'infinite' means, right?

Or are we getting cheated on this definition too?

Nope. This is the real deal.

The Hebrew interlinear reads, **'l'thbunth'u ain msphr'**.

Translation?

'... to understanding of Him, there is *no numbering'*!

Of course, the years of any age of time, even millenia long, can be numbered.

We must ask ourselves. Why didn't the Holy Spirit (and the men He inspired to write scripture) use **'*ain msphr'*** to describe humanity's time in Hell?

In point of fact, Petavel chronicles over *seventy* uses of **'eternal'** in the Bible that are 'objects of a temporary and limited nature'.[71]

Why then, are *aion* and *olam* not being translated plainly and correctly as **'age'** or **'eon'** or even **'world'**, in favor of *eternity, forever,* etc..?

A WORLD OF DIFFERENCE

What is it about this word **'*world'*** that Wycliffe uses in place of **'eon'**, or **'age'**?

Is he just getting this one wrong?

Go ahead and say the word *world* out loud.

Is it one or two syllables?

In Wycliffe's day, *world* was actually spelled *weorulde*, made up of two parts synonymous with 'age' or 'eon'

Weor was taken from the Latin *vir*, as in virile, an attribute of man.

Actually, the word 'werewolf' is a composite of this:

wer (man) + wolf= *man-wolf*.

The second half of 'weorulde' is *ald*, or *elde*, which means age or generation.

Hence, weor (man) + ulde (generation)= generation of man.

This is an *age*, or *eon*.

Literary use of *World* wasn't employed in the sense of 'the earth' until the thirteenth century.

It had always been a synonym for 'age' or 'eon'.

For instance, see if you can spot the trend in Ephesians 3.21,

'Unto him be glory in the church by Christ Jesus throughout all ages, world without end' (KJV).

The suffix **'without end'** was often tacked on after **'world'** around this time, as 'eternity' was being superimposed over *eon*.

It was at this time we see these words morph into something they had never been before.

Watch how the text devolves over time.

HANDLE WITH CARE

The NASB reads, **'to Him be the glory in the church and in Christ Jesus to all generations [a] forever and ever. Amen.'**

The verse is footnoted with '[a] literally- *of the age of the ages*'.

Wycliffe, a master of the original languages, understood this.

His translation reads, 'in to alle the generaciouns of the worldis'.

This is limited, not eternal.

William Tyndale, inspired by Wycliffe, also stayed true to the essence of the text, 'thorowout all generacions from tyme to tyme'.

Again- limited, not eternal.

But as the scriptures emerged from the darkness of their keepers, others were a little less careful in their zeal.

Coverdale (1535) has 'at all times for ever and ever.'

The Genevan (1557) has 'throughout all generations forever.'

The Rheims (1582) has 'unto al generations world without end.'

SLIPPERY SLOPE

It's believed that one reason for the slippery slope was the Vulgate's curious rendering of Exodus 15.18, 'The Lord shall reign *into eternity and beyond*'! (*in aeturnum et ultra*).

The rendering of this passage left some men scratching their heads.

The Hebrew text itself cautiously limits this reign 'to the eon, and further', as it describes an indefinite period of time which may or may not be eternal.

Clearly, there is no further to go past an endless eternity.

Eternity isn't the correct rendering in the first place!

By definition, there is nothing **'beyond'** eternity.

Wycliffe remained calm.

He understood the concept of *eons* in Hebrew and in the early Church.

He translated Exodus 15.8, 'The Lord schal regne [shall reign] in to the world, and ferth'e [further]'.[72]

This concept of the ages has always meant 'obscure' and 'beyond the horizon'.

The absolutism of eternity crept in later, as we'll see now.

BATTEN DOWN THE LATIN

Even before the time of Christ, the Roman Empire held sway over the known world.

Slowly over the centuries, the Caesars conquered lands from the Atlantic Ocean and across the Middle East.

At the height of their power, they ruled all the territories of the Greek monarch Alexander the Great, and then some.

At the time Alexander had supremacy over all these regions, he felt that every subject of the great Empire must be made to learn spoken Greek, and adopt Greek culture.

And this he did.

This policy was known as *Hellenism*.

Every province under his dominion was soon 'Hellenized' to speak and write *Koine*, common Greek used in trade and everyday life.

So intensive was this mandate, that several hundred years later Greek was still being used almost everywhere throughout the Roman Empire.

In fact, we see that the apostle Paul writes his letter to the Romans not in Latin, but in *Greek!*

But among the highborn elite of Rome, *Latin* was spoken and written (a good memory trick is to remember that you've probably heard Roman numerals also referred to as *Latin* numerals).

In the centers of learning and wealth, the privileged aristocrats corresponded by Latin contracts, Latin history, and, yes... Latin copies of scripture.

COMMUNICATION BREAKDOWN

But with the Phoenician *(aka Punic)* wars of the second and third centuries B.C., the North African territories of Egypt, Mauritania, Corsica, etc... were seized to also become the mistress of Rome.

There, the great schools of Carthage and Alexandria now largely taught- *Latin.*

However, separated from Rome by the vast Mediterranean Sea, the Latin spoken and written by these Romans of varied races and cultures began to drift widely from the precision of European Latin.

The result?

The language unraveled from the impeccable diction of Rome into any number of loose dialects that resembled one another less and less.

Polybius, Horace and other historians of the day stated frankly that the simple reading of a former treaty between Carthage and Rome drawn up one hundred years before was at best- difficult, and at worst- unreadable.

Quintillian (born A.D. 40) remarked that the Salian priests could hardly follow the sacred hymns.[73]

It fell to Tertullian (A.D. 160-220), and then Jerome (A.D. 347-420) to take the various manuscripts floating around, and to whittle them down to their strictest Latin form.

Jerome's finished work became known as the Vulgate, and held the field for nearly *one thousand years* through the Dark Ages, until the Protestant Reformation.

TO INFINITY AND BEYOND

England's culture and language was described as 'a melting pot' at this time.

In A.D. 1066, the Norman barbarians invaded and crushed England, and brought with them Danish, French and corroded Latin from Scandinavia.

Some later referred to this period as a 'wild anarchy of speech'.[74]

It was an uncomfortable time for Roman Church leaders in the age of Renaissance.

While Rome had kept the scriptures tightly under lock and key for centuries, and formalized all church proceedings in Latin ritual, men like Wycliffe (A.D. 1320-1384) dared to take the Vulgate and translate it for the vast majority of Englishmen who *didn't* know Latin (most of them).

Guess what he found.

Words Jerome had done his best to capture were now caught in the current of culture and progress swirling in England, and throughout Europe.

Two words in particular emerged- *seculum* and *aeturnus*.

OPTIMAL ILLUSION

Wycliffe was a picky and demanding scholar.

Unlike less attentive men after him, Wycliffe tried to practice the same care Jerome had as he carefully pored over the Vulgate.

The linguist Alexander Thomson wrote of Jerome.

'[I]n his revision, while correcting obvious errors and setting right what seemed to be bad Latin, was very conservative otherwise. Many expressions he left as he found them. Whatever may have been his own views regarding the future, he does not appear to have revised two Latin words, fraught with profound significance, which he found in the old version. These are both words used to render the Greek word eon, as Latin, like Gothic and Armenian and English, found two words necessary, *seculum*, from which we have our word "secular", and *aeturnus*, from which descended the fateful words "eternal" and "eternity"'.[75]

SECULUM

Latin dictionaries define *seculum* as a generation, an age, the world, the times and a period of one hundred years, but nowhere is it understood as eternal.

Its equal in French, *siècle*, has come to mean 'a century'.

In any case, it has always meant 'a long period of time'.

Hence, its usage as *'eon'*.

But as eons blurred into eternities, so was *seculum* misused.

Was there any precedent for an eternal *seculum*?

In one of his essays written around A.D. 160, Tertullian referred to 'a mighty shock impending over the entire world, and the conclusion of the *seculum* itself.'

Clearly, he wrote of the conclusion of the *age*, not the conclusion of eternity.

By its very nature, eternity never concludes.

Likewise, Eusebius recounts the trial of certain African believers in the year A.D. 180.

Unflinching before the interrogators of the proconsul, their leader Speratus answered the court, 'The empire of this *seculum* [world], I do not recognize.'

Surprisingly, they were granted thirty days to reconsider their statement, but Speratus did not waver, 'In a matter so straightforward there is no reconsideration'.

They were executed.

And Eusebius remarked that the martyrs would reign with God through 'all the *seculums* of the *seculums.*'

If seculum is to be read 'eternity', how does this account not defy the most basic logic?

Speratus was not testifying before the court of *eternity*, but of this world, of course.

And Eusebius was certainly not making an observation as senseless as this.

He was expressing the concept of the rest of time with 'all the *ages of the ages*', not 'all the *eternities of the eternities*'!

LET THE GAMES BEGIN... AND *END!*

Near the end of the second century, the historian Herodian noted the periodic games held in ancient Rome- 'secular games'.

Writing in Greek, these were recorded as *eonian* games. Obviously, these games were not eternal, but periodic.

Finally, listen to this.

The well-known Council of Trent convened in the sixteenth century to discuss various matters.

One of these was the notoriety of Jerome's Vulgate text.

It was here decreed, 'This same ancient and Vulgate edition, which by the long use of so many centuries has been approved in the Church itself, is to be held authentic in public readings, disputations, sermons and expositions; and no one is to dare or presume to reject it under any pretext whatever.'

Guess which word is used here for 'centuries'; *saeculorum*.

Seculums.

In defense of their manuscript locked away in a tower, they themselves actually provide a pretext here why it *should* be questioned.

Here they correctly use *seculum* in a statement defending a text using *seculum* incorrectly!

Yet *'no one is to dare or presume to reject it under any pretext whatever'!*

The Vulgate was not in use for 'so many *eternities*', let alone for even one eternity.

In point of fact, there is not one instance of *seculum* used to describe endless time.

AETURNUS

As we saw earlier, the Hebrew and Syriac equals of *aeturnus* were defined as 'beyond the horizon' and 'obscure'.

Of *aeturnus*, Thomson comments:

'Whatever the Latin word meant in the time of Jerome, it certainly did not signify *endless* three hundred years earlier. Professor Max Muller said of the root of this word, that it originally signified life or time, but had given rise to a number of words expressing eternity, the very opposite of life and time. He says the Latin *aevum* (which corresponds almost letter for letter with the Greek *aion*, eon, thought to have been originally *aivon*), became the name of time, age, and its derivative *aeviternus*, or *aeturnus*, "was made to express eternity." These are the words of an authority who was quite unbiased in this matter'.[76]

In keeping with this vague sense of the unknown, Phavorinus stated in the renowned 16th century volume of Greek words *Etymologicum*

Magnum, '...*aion* is the imperceptible (*aidios*) and the unending (*ateleuteetos*), as it seems to the theologian!'

Ah, touché Phavorinus!

Here, he takes a jab at the theology of men trying to cut a new and unintended facet into a stone long set for centuries.

Imperceptible doesn't necessarily mean unending!

For it was men like Cicero (1st century B.C.) and Ovid (1st century A.D.) who used *aeturnus* in their writings to refer to both *springtime* and *war*, neither of which go on forever, but for a long indefinite period of time.

Thomsen had more to say on this.

'As the word eon is really a transliteration of the Greek *aion*, its nearest English equivalent may be found in the word "age". The origin of this word is very interesting. It traces its descent back to the Latin *aevum*, which is the equivalent of the Greek *aion*. *Aevum* produces *aevitas*, which became shortened to *aetas*. From this was formed another form, *aetaticum*, a low Latin term. In France this was slurred into *edage*, then into *aage*, which arrived in England as *age*.'[77]

Now- who recalls how and when this word found its way into England?

Remember the barbarians of Normandy sweeping in from northern Europe, conquering and settling there?

Yep- A.D. 1066.

GHOSTS OF GREECE

Thomsen continues:

'So long as the Greek language was well understood in Italy, so long would *aionian* retain its force as meaning "eonian", and not only so, but it would tend to keep its Latin equivalent *aeturnum* tied down to the same signification'.

True.

The Greek language had evaporated from England, Italy and the known world.

Without the firm stanchion of Greek, Latin could not be tethered to it, and men began to pull it away.

Providentially, it was in the year 1453 that the great city of Constantinople was torn down in a siege by the Turks.

The force of the largest cannons ever made at that time were unleashed against the walls of the ancient capital, and massive sections of its walls were caved in by the barrage of immense shot slung from enormous catapults pitched outside.

How is this pertinent?

Constantinople (now known as Istanbul) was the great center of learning in the Middle East.

Legions of scholars warned of Turkish assault fled wast before the siege with everything they could carry.

Many hundreds of learned men scattered throughout Europe with original Greek texts of scripture.

While almost no Greek is found in European literature through the Middle Ages, we see the first Greek grammar in a thousand years published in Milan in 1476, and the first lexicon in 1480.

Just four years later, Greek was being taught publicly at Oxford University.

The Dutch scholar Erasmus mastered Greek, and became Professor of Greek at Cambridge.

Greek, and its original biblical text, began to be taught all across Europe.

One scholar remarked, 'Greece had arisen from the grave with the New Testament in her hand'! [78]

But by now, 'eternity' had slipped in by hasty revision.

If the first European translators had the Greek text to work from, we would likely be discussing *ages* today instead of eternity.

But what we have was translated from Latin copies, and *eternity* worked itself into our modern thinking.

HOLD YOUR FIRE

'WHY does it matter?' someone is saying, *'What does this all mean?'*

It means a great deal.

Tell me:

Is there any difference between **'everlasting punishment'** (RSV) and **'punishment lasting for an age'** (YLT)?

We must admit that only *one* of these translations is technically correct.

Is it possible that when men are sent to the lake of fire that there may be an *end* to their torment, and their existence?

The implications are enormous.[79]

And let's remember.

Ultimately, it doesn't matter what any of us would *like* God's word to say.

It simply says what it says.

Now what does scripture tell us about God's *character?*

CHAPTER 14:

PRIEST OR BEAST?

A young lady couldn't help but notice the old timer and his grandson in the same grocery aisle.

Having spotted a box of cookies, the toddler howled and strained his little body as Grandpa patiently rolled the cart on by, "It won't be much longer, Kenny. Just a few aisles left."

By the tone of his shrieking, she could tell the boy was determined to have the juice he had spied in the next aisle.

Grandpa reassured calmly, "Easy there, Kenny. Not long now."

Finally, she noticed that the candy bars at the checkout counter were just out of the lad's reach- and he was sure to let everyone in the store know it.

The old timer could barely be heard over the youngster's wailing, "We're real close here, Kenny. Two minutes, and we'll be heading home for a bottle, and a nap."

In the parking lot, the young lady paused to encourage the old gentleman, "I just wanted to compliment you on your patience with little Kenny here."

"Oh, that's Jerry," he sighed, *"I'm Kenny!"*

A MOTHER'S LOVE

We've all seen tantrums in public.

I've seen three years olds scream as loud as a human being is physically able in the aisle of a store. I'm guessing you might have too.

For the most part, we understand that a good parent does their best to model and expect reasonable behaviors, and sacrifices for the good of the child.

But some parents aren't good.

Imagine a father who arbitrarily singles out one daughter for cold isolation in the basement, neglect or abuse for… any reason at all.

Deep in their hearts, just how good might the other two children really believe Dad is, if this be the case?

In his book *A Child Called 'It'*, Dave Pelzer relates a sickening account of his childhood in such a home.

From an early age, it was made clear to Dave that he was not actually a part of the family.

Starvation for up to two weeks at a time was routine. Dave, however, was expected to wash all of their dishes after their every meal; if he was caught snatching a morsel of food during cleanup, he was forced to vomit, and later- eat what he had thrown up.

After his chores were completed, he was dismissed to a cold garage, where he was expected to stand in place. Sitting or leaning was forbidden, the penalty for which might be eating the baby's dirty diaper, or a spoonful of bleach. There, he tried to rest on an old Army cot, while the family slept in their own beds upstairs, warm and peaceful.

He went to the bathroom in a bucket.

Even uglier than the physical starvation Dave endured was the *social* starvation.

He was not to be spoken to, or touched. He was simply permitted to carry out his menial tasks, as a servant. He was not called brother or son. If he was not being given orders, he was not addressed. When Dave happened to hear the family speaking about him, he was to be referred to as 'the boy', or 'It'.

If all this psychological abuse wasn't sick enough, perhaps most disturbing was the fact that Dave was there to look on while his brothers were spoken with, and hugged, and commended.

Even more insidious, they were warned that if *they* ever treated Dave like a member of the family, they may also be missing meals and sleeping in the garage with him.[80]

Is God that kind of Father?

HELL TO PAY

Hear heavyweight theologian F.F. Bruce.

'Eternal conscious torment is incompatible with the revealed character of God.'[81]

Let me repeat that observation:

'Eternal conscious torment is incompatible with the revealed character of God.'

Among the range of doctrinal positions, there are those who believe that God has chosen many millions of human beings to be locked into an unchangeable life of oppression in the darkness of earth, to go directly into the darkness of unending Hell.

The idea that our God, **'the Father of mercies, and the God of all comfort'** (2 Co 1.3) will sweep billions of blind illiterate souls into Hellfire for eons upon eons *ad infinitum*, gnawed by immortal worms and scalded in a pitch black inferno never set perfectly well with me.

Not because it wasn't in keeping with my doctrine.

It was.

And as far as I could tell, it was in keeping with God's Word.

It just didn't seem to be in keeping with God's heart.

Inevitably, we were challenged with the logical question.

"So God chooses people to burn in Hellfire for eternity, and they have no say in it?"

Like the radio pastor we met in our Introduction, we could only steel our resolve to repeat what we were told, *"God is just, and He knows best".*

Certainly He is, and does.

I still believe that with all of my heart.

But I'm not convinced that men got this one doctrine infallibly irrefutably right.

We've covered that journey throughout this book

If predestination to eternal torture is the inevitability of most people on earth, who could fault Dave's mother for child abuse?

If anything, she's to be applauded for helping David mentally prepare for the likelihood of Hell. Utter helplessness at the hand of a fickle parent who ignores and threatens and terrorizes his own children as the mood may take him.

From this perspective, Dave's mother has done no worse than God Himself.

In point of fact, it could be said that she was simply showing Dave another aspect of love.

Character formation.

If eternal torment is an unchangeable fact, then we, like Dave's siblings, are left with a profound storm of foreboding in our hearts.

Is this love?

THE FAIREST OF THEM ALL

Philosopher and skeptic Robert G. Ingersoll had this to say.

'[W]hen the great ship freighted with mankind goes down in the night of death, chaos and disaster, I am willing to go down with the ship... If there is a God who will damn his children forever, I would rather go to hell than to go to heaven and keep the society of such an infamous tyrant. I make my choice now. I despise that doctrine. It has covered the cheeks of this world with tears. It has polluted the hearts of children, and poisoned the imaginations of men... This doctrine never should be preached again. What right have you, sir, Mr. clergyman, to stand at the portals of the tomb, at the vestibule of eternity, and fill the future with horror and with fear? I do not believe this doctrine: neither do you. If you did, you could not sleep one moment. Any man who believes it, and has within his breast a decent, throbbing heart, will go insane.'[82]

Thank you, Ingersoll. You're right.

He was a passionate observant man, as many lost men may be.

In no uncertain terms, he made it clear that he was nauseously grieved at the prospect of human beings roasting in endless flames.

Who wouldn't be?

In any case, his visceral reaction to it wasn't enough to guide him to Jesus.

And why should it?

Ingersoll's revulsion for the doctrine of Eternal Torment developed into revulsion for Christ, and His Church.

He makes a nakedly clear point.

For those who are convinced that all who reject Christ will burn in Hellfire for eternity- why have we not shared this impending doom with every unsaved person we know?

I don't know about you. I haven't.

There's a reason for that.

As Ingersoll said, we don't likely believe it.

We're ashamed.

We profess to believe this awful woe upon all mankind, but we can hardly bring ourselves to share it with those so many around us destined to endless Hellfire.

We may have told people about a God who loves them, but the part about what He will do to them if they decline is the tough part.

Is that tougher than burning forever?

THE SLUMS of HEAVEN

We're hesitant to go there.

While Ingersoll may have directed his comments more to the world, Emmanuel Petavel aimed his at the Church, and pulled no punches.

'It [*eternal torment*] must be loyally proclaimed or else denounced. If believed, it should be preached from the housetops; if not believed, it should be opposed to the very end. If this dogma be false, it is a calumny [lie] against God and a stumbling-block in the way of humanity'[83]

Eternal torment is either a fact or a fallacy.

It can only be one, or the other.

And if it is a fact, it is *the* most pivotal fact the lost need to hear, that they may have some chance to avoid it.

OF DOGS AND MEN

Imagine telling a number of Christians about what goes on in a dog-fighting ring.

Those who run them claim the animals are 'bred mean'.

Even so, when we hear about the pain these dogs are subjected to, we're appalled.

Rightly so.

I can taste the outrage now.

Now imagine telling those same Christians about billions of human beings subjected to the ultimate agony- *forever*.

We can almost be sure of a more tepid response.

Why?

There is a disconnect.

Believe it or not, Jesus spoke to this religious tendency to downplay humanity.

'How much more valuable then is a man than a sheep!'   Mt 12.12

In Luke, He said **'you are more valuable than many sparrows.'**   12.7

Further, how much more agonizing is the pain of Hellfire than the skirmish of two dogs?

And how much longer is eternity than the dogs' last minutes of contest?

Incomparable, of course.

FINAL EXAM

The *gravity* of eternal torment demands that it be reexamined.

To that point, we must set aside the concept of **'eternal'** from the word *torment* itself.

The word *torment* is never employed in scripture in regard to the Judgment.

THE SLUMS of HEAVEN

Without His permission, men slapped this term on their interpretation of God's treatment of the lost.

Imagine if every violator of every law, from grand theft to rolling through a red light, to murder to spitting on the sidewalk were each shoved into a gruesome little crypt to be tortured for the rest of their lives.

Not forever- just for their remaining time on earth.

Some older lawbreakers would only suffer five or ten years of agony.

Younger culprits might face 40, 50, 60, 70 years of the worst treatment on earth- physical and psychological torture in captivity.

I'm sure we can all agree that would be *recklessly* unjust.

Here in the United States, that would qualify as the worst form of *'cruel and unusual punishment'*, according to the Eighth Amendment of our Constitution.

Abroad, such men are arrested for *'crimes against humanity'*, as they should be.

Now multiply that penalty by trillions of centuries.

AN EYE FOR AN EYE

The problem here, of course, is that this veers so wildly from even God's *Old* Covenant guidelines for behavior towards enemies.

Thomas Talbot comments:

'Contrary to popular belief, the Old Testament principle of retaliatory justice- 'an eye for an eye and a tooth for a tooth'- was never instituted for the purpose of justifying harsh punishment for serious crimes, something that no one at the time would have questioned; instead it was instituted for the purpose of *eliminating excessive punishment*, such as capital punishment in exchange for a tooth.' (emphasis mine)[84]

This is known as the principle of equal retaliation (*lex talionis*).

It served its purpose well.

Let's imagine a fellow who might be tempted to kick a woman in the ribs and steal her moneybag.

Certainly, the fellow's forethought of his own broken ribcage was a deterrent, in some cases.

This makes sense.

But more than that, the woman out of a fair amount of money, feeling violated and wincing under the pain of a fractured rib, could not call for the thief's death by stoning.

THE GOOD, THE BAD & THE UGLY

Did you know that Jesus actually cites this verse, and *redefines it*?

He says, **'You have heard that it was said, 'AN EYE FOR AN EYE, AND A TOOTH FOR A TOOTH.'**

But I say to you, do not resist an evil person.'　　　　　Mt 5.38-39

Essentially, He was saying 'The Law gave you the equal balance of cruelty for the crime. But don't feel you *need* to strike back. You don't.'

A few verses later, he expands on that.

'You have heard that it was said, 'YOU SHALL LOVE YOUR NEIGHBOR and hate your enemy.' [44] But I say to you, love your enemies and pray for those who persecute you, so that you may be sons of your Father who is in heaven... Therefore you are to be perfect, as your heavenly Father is perfect.'

Mt 5.43-48

Love your enemies... as your heavenly Father.

Again, Jesus says in so many words, 'The Old Covenant was a basic guideline. But you can do even better. You can be like the Father, and give mercy freely, with all your heart'.

Having now read this, is it probable that our Father stokes endless Hellfire to torture those who reject Him?

Is this a just sentence for those who neglect Christ?

Is this what we can expect from the Father?

MODUS OPERANDI?

Let's overview these:

Moses: Don't inflict punishment any worse than what they have done to you.

Jesus: Don't inflict punishment at all- forgive.

Jesus, later: I will inflict endless punishment in Hellfire on those who turn away from Me.

Is this likely?

His own metaphor had been clear.

'But these enemies of mine, who did not want me to reign over them, bring them here and *slay* them in my presence.'   Lk 19.27

They were slain.

Their lives were ended.

Torture is reserved for other parables, but not here.

Does anyone see an inconsistency here?

Is He really saying, '*While we're on earth, we'll turn the other cheek, and forgive seventy times seven, etc... But just wait. Once we get on the other side, that all changes. I will personally sentence them to torture by Hellfire and worms that will never end, even though they still know not what they do'.*

Clark H. Pinnock had this to say, 'Surely a God who would do such a thing would be more nearly like Satan than like God... Is this not a most disturbing concept which needs some second thoughts?... Does the One who told us to love our enemies intend to wreak vengeance on His own enemies for all eternity?'[85]

YOUR LAST REQUEST: BREAD OR STONE?

Rightly, some argue, "This is *anthropomorphism* (attributing human characteristics to a deity, animal or object)! *We can't assume that God will be as kind as people expect Him to be, just because people want kindness! Yes, people can be nice- but that's just taking human traits, and slapping them on God. He is God!"*

Absolutely, He is- He alone.

And certainly the themes of Almighty King and Judge are there in scripture, even in the New Testament.

And yet at times, Christ Himself set God and man alongside one another.

In Matthew, He asks, **'what man is there among you who, if his son asks for bread, will give him a stone? Or if he asks for a fish, will he give him a serpent? If you then, being evil, know how to give good gifts to your children,** *how much more* **will your Father who is in heaven give good things to those who ask Him!'** 7.9-11

Simply, Jesus says, 'I Myself *put* this essence of benevolence in humanity. I made Moms and Dads to have this innate indescribably deep love and concern for their own children. This is universal. *How much more* can *you* expect that from Me?'

This model of God's affection and care is on display in homes across the earth.

It is a witness of His kindness by design.

On the other hand, Christ likened rigor under the rule of religious men to forced labor, **'they bind heavy burdens, hard to bear, and lay them on men's shoulders.'** Mt 23.4

Again, He Himself offers hope.

He reassured them, **'I am gentle and humble in heart, and you will find**

rest for your souls.

For my yoke is easy and my burden is light.'   Mt 11.29-30

Yet again, men have often sharpened and complicated God's simple way, as we saw in Chapters 4 through 10.

MIDNIGHT SNACK

Luke records a parable Jesus tells of a man appealing to his own neighbor for bread for a tired guest.

The man's answer:

'Don't bother me. The door is already locked, and my children and I are in bed. I can't get up and give you anything.'   Lk 11.7

The truth is, he was *already* up out of bed, talking through the door.

Helping his neighbor would have been as simple as throwing the bolt back, and handing a couple of pieces of bread to him.

Bottom line: *'I will not help you'*.

But God says, *'I will'*, as if to say, essentially, 'Men will treat you unkindly, but you should not form your opinion of Me from their cruelty or indifference.'

That said, I don't want this aspect of God's kindness to be mistaken for the Church's generally low view of God's strength and sovereignty, either.

I think we've all seen this tendency to hold God to some soft human moral standard. That's always bothered me.

For some, this is the dichotomy.

SPLIT PERSONALITY?

'God is love' (1 Jn 4.8), and yet **'He is just'** (Dt 32.4, DRA).
'He does what is right and fair' (GNT).

The fact that God pardons magnanimously doesn't need to mean that He is a feeble distracted pushover. I reject this caricature.

On the contrary, He is supremely full of raw universal power and wisdom to judge- forever. And judge He will.

At the same time, **'He delights in mercy.'**   Mc 7.18

It is His *delight* and His nature to forgive.

Would it be fair for us to ask?

'Will God oversee the eternal torment of billions in Hellfire?'

MOVING THE STRIKE ZONE

Let's take this thought into the New Testament.

Jesus told those born again believers in Laodicea that they did not *know* that they were **'wretched, and miserable, and poor, and blind, and naked.'**   Re 3.17

But **'He knows our frame; He remembers we are dust.'**   Ps 103.14

Of course, He has the right to sentence humanity to any fate- even

THE SLUMS of HEAVEN

endless torture in Hellfire, worms, etc...

Despite twenty plus years of being taught no other doctrine, I now find Eternal Torment difficult to see in scripture, or reason, or history.

Some hold the opinion that *"If we loosen the teaching of eternal torment in Hell, the blood of Christ will be cheapened!"*

Simply, Jesus' blood is the most precious thing that's ever touched the earth, period.

That point is sure and immovable, regardless of whether or not a man goes into Hell briefly, or for eternity.

Frankly, the duration of a man's punishment is irrelevant.

We might expect this cheapening to be a reasonable conclusion if eternal torment is established in scripture.

I don't believe it is.

In my opinion, a non sequitur.

How so?

Rewind to... let's say A.D. 1120.

In order to please God, a man resolves to be a monk.

PENANCE VERSUS PRESENCE

Many a man entering the monastery believed that God was very angry with him.

They were told that they could deflect some of that wrath by a daily commitment to many hours of prayer along the rosary beads, fasting and silence.

To flay ones' own skin with a whip, or to sleep naked out in the cold, or better yet- on a bed of nails- was said to alleviate even more of God's displeasure.

While some may think or live this way, I myself don't see any of this in scripture.

And yet, this mindset was woven deeply into the fabric of monastic life and culture.

To prefer to sleep in a bed with a blanket was seen by some to be unholy pride against God.

Is it?

Some have also decided that any step away from Eternal Torment must be sacrilege, as it is exponentially less severe, and therefore must be an attempt to water down 'the hard truth'.

Eternal torment is often seen as the fastball down the middle.

I have to disagree.

As I see it, the evidence points to men having moved the strike zone.

AND BEHIND DOOR # 3...

We've examined biblical (and extra biblical) texts, apocalyptic symbolism, history, etymology and logic.

To me, the evidence leads strongly in the direction of Conditionalism.

There is no shortage of resources in favor of other positions. I've read many.

But may we now reconsider.

Universalism seems to sit on the far end of the spectrum. It would appear to offer little or no justice for those violated in this life.

And those lives are precious. God knows that infinitely greater than you and I.

On the other far end of the spectrum Traditionalists insist, sometimes begrudgingly, that every soul who declines Jesus' offer will burn in endless agony.

The misery will never end. They will never have a way out of continual torture.

Through the research presented here, I am compelled to conclude that the real truth lies somewhere between these two extremes.

There's a reason why this notion of Eternal Torment seems so unlike God's heart.

We don't actually believe it came from God's heart, but from men's.

'The LORD is compassionate and gracious,
Slow to anger and abounding in lovingkindness.
9 He will not always strive with us,
Nor will He keep His anger forever.
10 He has not dealt with us according to our sins,
Nor rewarded us according to our iniquities.'   Ps 103.8-10

APPENDIX 1:

THE ETERNITY WITH A BEGINNING

This Appendix is a must-read. A masterful, concise record of the forging of scripture, Alexander Thomson breaks it down from the early centuries through the Renaissance.

A tireless scholar and editor, Thomson worked with the translators of the *Concordant Literal Version* of the Bible, providing corrections. The following lengthy excerpt is cited from his work, Whence Eternity, published in 1935:

'Some of the following facts may at first sight seem somewhat startling, yet that is because they are not widely known. Had the old English Bibles been translated direct out of the Greek, instead of from the Latin Vulgate Version of Jerome (380 A.D.), it is very probable that the word eternal would never have been found in our modern Bibles and theological terminology at all. But for the Norman Conquest of England in 1066 A.D., which brought many French words into the English language (and French is largely decayed and corrupt Latin), and drove out many native English words, we should most probably now be using not eternal, but ece, the old equivalent of eonian. On the other hand, had the sack of Constantinople by hordes of Turks from Asia taken place prior to the Norman Conquest, instead of in 1453, the likelihood is that we should have had the Greek term eonian incorporated into English, instead of the Latin eternal. The capture of Constantinople by the Turks was of enormous importance to Europe. It was then the great center of learning, especially Greek learning, When it was sacked, hosts of learned doctors were scattered abroad all over Europe, carrying with them the knowledge of the Greek tongue and the treasures of Greek literature.

'It is hard to believe that for over a thousand years, up till the year 1453, Greek was almost unknown or forgotten in most of Europe. Even in Italy, which formerly had been dominated by Greek, it became almost unknown. Very few quotations from Greek poets are to be found in Italian writers from the sixth to the fourteenth centuries. No Greek was taught publicly in England until about 1484, when it began to be taught at Oxford University. Erasmus, the great Dutch scholar, learnt Greek at Oxford and subsequently was Professor of Greek at Cambridge from 1509 till 1514, during which time Tyndale studied there. Erasmus issued his first Greek New Testament in 1516. This was the first Greek New Testament printed for sale. The first Greek grammar for well over a thousand years was published at Milan in 1476, and the first lexicon four years later. As an English scholar expressed it, "Greece had arisen from the grave with the New Testament in her hand." About this time great German scholars even changed their names to Greek ones, so fashionable had the study of Greek become. Schwartzerd (black earth) became Melanchthon; Hausschein (house-shine) was discarded for Oecolampadius; Gerhard attained fame as Erasmus; Horn took on more dignity as Ceratinus.

HOW THE LATIN LANGUAGE AFFECTED THEOLOGY

THE SLUMS of HEAVEN

'In order to understand aright the word "eternal," it is necessary to make a review of linguistic conditions in Greece and Italy before and after the days of Paul.

'The classical Latin tongue was one out of many that were spoken by the early inhabitants of Italy. At first it was only the dialect of a small area around Rome. Other dialects which in the course of time mingled with it were of a very different type, such as the Etruscan. Many colonies of Greeks existed in early times in the south of Italy, so that this part was known as "Great Greece." From the dawn of authentic history the Greek language may be seen exerting a strong influence over Italy. When in B.C. 454 the Romans desired to establish a code of laws, they dispatched commissioners to Greece to study and report upon the laws of Solon at Athens. What in later times became the polished dialect of the district of Latium was not the language of the common people, just as the classical Greek of the poets and dramatists was not the common speech of the people. The everyday language of Greeks was much the same as is found in the Greek Scriptures, known as the koinee, or "common," or vulgar tongue. Latin was the speech of the patricians, of the literary world, of the politicians.

'One effect of the rapid conquests of Alexander the Great (B.C. 334-323) was that Greek became the language of government and literature throughout most of the then civilized world. It became the *lingua franca* of countries such as Palestine and Egypt. About the year B.C. 280 Rome was mistress of all Italy except some of the Greek cities in the south. These succumbed by B.C. 276. Sixty years later Rome was interfering in the affairs of Greece itself, and by B.C. 189 Rome was mistress of Greece.

'Nevertheless, Greek continued to be the fashionable speech in Italy for a long time. In the time of Dionysius Thrax (about B.C. 80), the children of gentlemen in Rome learnt Greek before they learnt Latin. Dionysius was the author of the first Greek school grammar ever compiled in Europe, published in Rome in the time of Pompey (about B.C. 50), which became the basis of all subsequent Greek grammars, and was the book used in schools for centuries. This small and elementary work of only a few pages is still in existence. The first history of Rome was written at Rome in Greek by Fabius Pictor about B.C. 200.

In the first two centuries A.D., Greek was very generally used in Rome. In addition to Latin, numerous other dialects might be heard in the streets of Rome and throughout Italy, and the Greek language served as a common medium whereby all might communicate with each other. For this reason, there was no need for Paul to write his epistle to Rome in Latin. As he was much too sensitive to write to them in a tongue they would not understand, it is clear that the Roman church must have been quite at home with the Greek tongue. For a similar reason, there was no need for a Latin version of the Scriptures in Italy for about a hundred years after Paul's time. It is of profound significance to note, that when the first Latin version was made, it had its origin, not in Italy, but in North Africa. Of the manuscripts extant belonging to the Old Latin version, that is to say, the version in use before the time of Jerome (380 A.D.), the majority may be recognized as being of the "African" type.

It is here necessary to explain that what became the Roman province of "Africa" was in early times the Canaanite colony of Carthage, in North Africa, near Tunis. This colony was founded by the cities of Tyre and Sidon, and some have sought to identify Carthage with Tarshish (as the Greek version of Isa.23:1). Carthage ruled over the large islands of Sardinia and Corsica, and over part of Sicily also. Warfare with the rising military power of Rome was inevitable. Three long struggles, known as the Punic (or Phoenician) Wars, took place between B.C. 264 and 146, culminating in the complete subjugation of Carthage, which now became a province of Rome.

Henceforth the speech of this Roman colony was Latin, but it was the Latin dialect of about the middle of the second century B.C. This is important. The Latin dialect of this time was very different from what it became a hundred years later. Polybius, the Greek historian, states, about B.C. 150, that the best informed Romans of that time could not understand without difficulty the language of the former treaties entered into between Rome and Carthage, less than a hundred years before. Horace, who died about the time Christ was born, confessed that he could not understand the old Latin Salian poems, and he infers that Latin had so greatly changed within a few hundred years that no one else could understand them. Quintilian (born 40 A.D.) states that even the Salian priests could scarcely follow their sacred hymns. The purest era of Latin in Rome was during the hundred years before Christ came. It was then that the language became fixed and polished.

Carthage, however, being a colony, at a considerable distance from Rome, spoke a somewhat different Latin than did Rome. It was free from the influence of Greek. Just as the Scandinavian spoken in Norway and Sweden has diverged much from the old Scandinavian of a thousand years ago still spoken in Iceland; as the "taal" of the Boers in South Africa has diverged much from the Dutch of Holland; as the English carried to America three hundred years ago has preserved certain words and meanings and lost others, so the Latin transported to Carthage came in course of time to diverge, in certain respects, from the Latin spoken in Italy and Rome. As invariably happens in such cases, certain old expressions and nuances were preserved which died out elsewhere, while in other cases fresh nuances came into use.

It is to Tertullian, a Latin of Carthage, who lived from about 160 to 220 A.D., that we are indebted for our first knowledge of the existence of the Old Latin version of the Scriptures. He was the earliest of the Latin Fathers. The manuscripts of this version in existence show that the Latin employed was very different from classical Latin, being more vigorous, yet marked by solecisms (or improprieties in the language used-what would appear to others as errors in grammar and violations of syntax and idiom). It may have been originally a translation from the Greek made by comparatively illiterate people, or the language may be due simply to the differences in dialect between the Latin of Rome and the Latin of Carthage. So long as the Old Latin scriptures remained in North Africa, they continued with little or no change, but immediately they arrived on the soil of Italy, a great disturbance took place. Old words in use in Carthage were found to be unintelligible to the Romans, while new words coined there were not understood. Words in both countries had, in the course of two or three centuries, taken on distinctive and divergent nuances of their own. The provincial solecisms and roughnesses of the African version were patched up and corrected by means of the Greek version current in Italy, and in course of time the result came to be indescribable confusion. There were said to be as many versions as manuscripts, though this is no doubt somewhat of an exaggeration. Upon Jerome fell the arduous task of attempting to bring about harmony out of this confusion, and the outcome was his version of the Latin scriptures which in after times, from the thirteenth century onwards, was known as the "Vulgate." Hitherto, for about six hundred years, the Greek Septuagint version had held the field, and there was intense and prolonged opposition to Jerome's version. This was the Bible which was to dominate most of Christendom for a thousand years, right up to the Reformation. Jerome, however, in his revision, while correcting obvious errors and setting right what seemed to be bad Latin, was very conservative otherwise. Many expressions he left as he found them. Whatever may have been his own views regarding the future, he does not appear to have revised two Latin words, fraught with profound significance, which he found in the old version. These are both words used to render the Greek word eon, as Latin, like Gothic and Armenian and English, found two words necessary, *seculum*, from which we have our word "secular," and *aeternus*, from which have descended the fateful words "eternal" and "eternity."..

'We shall now examine the derivation of these two Latin words, one of which was destined to exercise such a profound influence over the minds of men for so long, an influence not in accord with truth, and by no means for the glory of God.

ETERNAL AND SECULAR

'Seculum is defined in Latin dictionaries as meaning a generation, an age, the world, the times, the spirit of the times, and a period of a hundred years. That which is secular pertains to the present world, especially to the world as not spiritual. In French the word has come to mean a century, besides meaning age, time, period, and world (*siecle*). The future *siecle* is the "life to come." In the French Bible, "for the eons of the eons" is rendered by "to the *siecles* of the *siecles*," following the Latin Vulgate. The other Romance languages follow the same construction, Italian using *secoli*, and Spanish *siglos*. Irish and Gaelic use *saoghal*, Roumanian uses *seculi*, and even Basque has *secula*...

'Seculum is sometimes derived from the same root that gives "sequel," meaning time as "following." Before the rise of words to express eternity, time was viewed as flowing onwards, generation following generation into the dim future. Others derive *seculum* from the root that gives section, as meaning time cut off, divided, or decided.

'Long ago in Rome, periodic games were held, which were called "secular" games. Herodian, the historian, writing in Greek about the end of the second or beginning of the third century, calls these "eonian" games. In no sense were the games eternal. Eonian did not mean eternal any more than a *seculum* meant eternity.

*[This is precisely the point; the games were *periodic*, marked by *divisions of time*, just the opposite of eternal]

'Among the many inscriptions in the Catacombs of Rome is one to the memory of a girl of fifteen years who had died. It is inscribed to "Aurelia, our sweetest daughter, who departed from the *seculum*" (or world,-*quae de saeculo recessit*). Some of the old Roman writers use the word in the sense of the utmost lifetime of man, a century. It may be said that every hundred years the race of man is completely changed. Some people change little within a generation, but after a hundred years the entire physical appearance of the race has altered.

'The famous Council of Trent, in Italy, sitting from 1545 to 1563, decreed that "This same ancient and Vulgate edition, which by the long use of so many centuries has been approved in the church itself, is to be held authentic in public readings, disputations, sermons and expositions; and no one is to dare or presume to reject it under any pretext whatever." The word used for "centuries" is *saeculorum*, seculums.

'Trajan, who was emperor of Rome from 98 to 117 A.D., wrote to Pliny regarding the conviction of those who professed the Christian faith. Such were not to be specially sought out or hunted, yet if accused and convicted must bear the punishment. He adds that accusations against them which were not signed were not to be accepted on any account, as this was the "very worst example that could be shown, and pertains not to our seculum."

'Tertullian, born about 160 A.D., in one of his many writings, referred to "a mighty shock impending over the entire world, and the conclusion of the *seculum* itself."

[Again,'the conclusion of the eternity'* is impossible. By the very nature of its meaning, it *cannot* 'conclude'. This is solid proof that the word was meant to be translated 'ages', as they end, while the essence of eternity *has no conclusion*.]

'Lactantius, born about 260 A. D., speaks of the "learned ones of this *seculum*." Eusebius, the historian of the early Church, born about 265 A.D., gives an account of the trial of certain martyrs from Africa in the year 180. The martyrs showed a most indomitable spirit when interrogated by the proconsul. Speratus, their leader, replied, "The empire of this seculum (world) I do not recognize." The proconsul pressed them to take thirty days to reconsider. Speratus replied, "In a matter so straightforward there is no reconsideration." Eusebius goes on to relate that the martyrs would reign with God through "all the*seculums* of the *seculums*."

*[Of course,'all the eternities (plural) of the eternities (plural) are exponentially redundant. Plural plurals of infinite numbers multiplied by infinite numbers. Clearly, 'ages' were meant here.]

'Writing about "Our Lord's Miracles," Eusebius alludes to "magicians who have ever existed throughout the*seculums*." This is a reference to past ages.

'These examples are sufficient to show that *seculum* was used very much as the Greek αιων. No case can be cited in which it, refers to endless time.

'We shall now consider its usage by Jerome in the Latin Vulgate Version. Those who maintain that the Greek αιων signifies eternity or "for ever" would do well to consider very carefully Jerome's renderings from Greek into Latin. Out of about 130 occurrences of eon in the Greek New Testament, Jerome renders by *seculum* 101 times, while he uses *aeternum* 27 times. If by the latter word he meant eternity, he is very inconsistent. It is to the Latin versions that we must look for the origin of the pernicious system, or rather lack of system, of giving to the Greek eon two diverse meanings. In every occurrence in the Unveiling, of the expression "for the eons of the eons," Jerome has, "for the seculums of the seculums," which Wiclif, with studied carefulness, rendered by "in to worldis of worldis," just as five hundred years before Wiclif's time the Old English glosses of Latin manuscripts gave "world" for *seculum*. The following are some of the expressions used by Jerome: "from the seculum," "from the seculums," "for the seculum," "for the seculums," "before the seculums," "this seculum," "that seculum," "the consummation of the seculum," "the consummation of the seculums," "the ends of the seculums," "in the seculum of the seculum," "the future seculum," "the coming seculum," "the impending seculums," "the seculum of this world." In Jude 25 he renders by, "before the entire seculum, and now, and for all the seculums of the seculums." Wiclif here has, "bifor alle worldis and now and in to alle worldis of worldis." Tyndale, coming one hundred and fifty years after Wiclif, has the utterly inadequate and bald and totally erroneous "now and for ever," although the Rheims version (1582 A.D.) has, "befoer al worldes, and now and for al worldes evermore."

*[Some are saying, 'Why "worlds" here? That's makes no better sense!' Consider that the meaning

of "world" has undergone great change since Wyclif's time.

'Our old word weorulde is composed of two distinct parts, and where the primitive pronunciation is preserved, two very distinct syllables are still heard. The former part of the word consists of wer, a man (like the Latin vir, as in virile, and the -er in words like speaker, also the wer- in werwolf, the man-wolf). The latter part of the word is ald, or elde, meaning age or generation. World is therefore defined as "the generation of men." That there is a close connection between the old word world and "eon" was beautifully shown by the old Gothic version, which, in 2 Tim.4: 10 has, for "this present world" (C.V. "the current eon"), the reading, tho nu ald, meaning, "this now age."'

We may need to be reminded here that an aion- 'eon' or 'age' is by definition a single, set, long yet limited period of time].

'In Eph.2:2, Jerome has "the seculum of this world" (C.V. "the eon of this world"). Wiclif did not understand this, and originated the guess, "the course of this world," which was slavishly copied by those who came after him.

'Turning to the Greek word eonian, which occurs seventy times in the New Testament, Jerome does not render about three quarters of them by the word secular, and one quarter by eternal, but no less than sixty-five times does he use the latter (aeternum), while secular he uses only twice (2 Tim.1:9 and Titus 1:2), "before times secular" (ante tempora saecularia). As forty-three of the seventy occurrences refer to life, he was unable to say, "secular life," and therefore invariably puts "eternal life."...

'An extraordinary surprise awaits us when we consider two verses wherein the Vulgate is, to say the least, bewildering. We have been reckoning the Latin in aeternum of Jerome's day as meaning "for eternity" or "into eternity," whatever it may have meant two or three hundred years before his time. It stands beyond all doubt that by seculum Jerome meant a limited period of time, an eon, but by aeternum he seems to have meant something different. Did he mean "eternity?" Or was this Latin word still used in the loose way it had been used long before his time, as meaning indefinite future time? Farrar says that even the Latin Fathers who had a competent knowledge of Greek knew that aeternum was used in the same loose way, for an indefinite period, in Latin writers, as (αιωνιον) was used in Greek. Exodus 15:18 reads in the A.V.: "The Lord shall reign for ever and ever." The Hebrew carefully limits this reign to "the eon and further." The Septuagint expands this into "the eon, and still more an eon, and further." Jerome astounds by actually rendering by "into eternity and beyond" (in aeternum et ultra). The same Latin reading is also found in Micah 4:5 (A.V. "We will walk in the name of the Lord our God for ever and ever.") where the Hebrew reads, "for the eon and further," and the Greek reads, "for the eon and beyond,"

'It is now necessary to examine the origin of the word "eternal." Whatever the Latin word meant in the time of Jerome, it certainly did not signify endless three hundred years earlier. Professor Max Muller said of the root of this word, that it originally signified life or time, but had given rise to a number of words expressing eternity, the very opposite of life and time. He says the Latin aevum (which corresponds almost letter for letter with the Greek αιων, eon, thought to have been originally aivon), became the name of time, age, and its derivative aeviternus, or aeternus, "was made to express eternity." These are the words of an authority who was quite unbiased in this matter.

198

'This statement resembles one made by Phavorinus in the sixteenth century in the famous "Etymologicum Magnum," a large tome giving the derivations of all Greek words, as handed down from a very much earlier time. The word αιων (eon) is defined, among other things, as "the life of mankind," and there is cited "the seven eons from the creation of the heaven and earth until the general resurrection of humanity." Phavorinus, the editor, adds "αιων is the imperceptible (*aidios*) and the unending (*ateleuteetos*), *as it seems to the theologian*!" What he meant was that originally the word never meant unending, but this meaning had been injected by theology. Indeed, he spoke truth, as it is theology, and theology alone, which in any language has imported into time-words the thought of endlessness.

'Before returning to the Latin, we shall cite one more similar yet very instructive case. The Emperor Justinian was the greatest of the Eastern (Byzantine) Emperors. He reigned from 527 to 565 at Constantinople. In the year 534 he published in fifty volumes the world famous "Justinian Code" of Laws. This was a digest of the Greek and Roman constitutions, ordinances, and legal decisions, culled from two thousand manuscript volumes, and it forms the basis of most medieval and modern codes of law. In the year 540, Justinian made arrangements for the calling together of the famous local council of four years later. He was determined that certain doctrines must be suppressed. In setting forth the position when writing to the Patriarch Mennas of Constantinople, he discussed the doctrines with great ability. In particular, he wished it made very plain that the life of the saints was to be everlasting, and that the doom of the lost was to be likewise. Yet he did not argue that the word eonian meant everlasting. Nor did he claim that the word eonian had hitherto been misunderstood. In setting forth the orthodox position of the Church of that time, he did not say, "We believe in *eonian* punishment," as this was exactly what Origen, three hundred years before, had maintained and believed. In fact, Origen, who exulted in the truth of the reconciliation of the universe, definitely used the word eonian with reference to fire and doom as meaning a limited time. But writing in the very expressive Greek language, Justinian says, "The holy church of Christ teaches an *endless eonian* (*ateleuteetos* αιωνιος) life for the just, and *endless* (*ateleuteetos*) punishment for the wicked." Justinian knew quite well that by itself eonian did not signify endless, and he therefore added a word the meaning of which is quite unequivocal, a word not found in the Scriptures. This letter of Justinian, which is still in existence, ought to convince anyone who is in doubt, regarding the true scriptural meaning of the word eonian..

'The old Latin writers used *aeternum* in the same sense as Greek writers used *aionion*, as meaning eonian. Thus Cicero, who died B.C. 43, says of the future, "Springtime will be *aeternum*," that is, enduring, eonian. At present springtime is brief, fleeting, seasonal. He was referring to a spring which will endure.. Ovid, who flourished about 9 A.D., speaks of warfare in the same sense.

'As the word eon is really a transliteration of the Greek *aion*, its nearest English equivalent may be found in the word "age." The origin of this word is very interesting. It traces its descent back to the Latin aevum, which is the equivalent of the Greek *aion*. *Aevum* produced *aevitas*, which became shortened to *aetas*. From this was formed another form, *aetaticum*, a Low Latin term. In France this was slurred into *edage*, then into *aage*, which arrived in England as *age*.

'How then, did the Latin *aeternum* and the Greek *aionion*, which both originally referred to that which is eonian, come to signify "eternal" in our modern sense? There is no doubt that these words have been "made to express" what is eternal, the instrument in every case being theology. The process seems to have been somewhat as follows.

'There have always been some among the sects who have held harsh views regarding the doom of the sinner. The Pharisees and the Essenes are said to have believed in conscious future punishment. The Essenes believed in unintermittent (*adialeipton*) and "deathless" punishment...

'The collapse of the truth of the eons left the way open for pagan error to re-assert itself and foist itself upon scripture teaching. So long as the Greek language was well understood in Italy, so long would aionion retain its force as meaning "eonian," and not only so, but it would tend to keep its Latin equivalent aeternum tied down to the same signification, in Italy. But an influence was arising in the second century in North Africa which was to change everything, and compel these terms to bear, in theology, a meaning they never had originally. It is more than probable that the Latin aeternum bore in North Africa a sense slightly divergent from what it bore in Rome. It may have signified not only "eonian," but something in addition, or something more vague. It seems by that time to have been coming to signify what it later signified everywhere, not only that which has no *seen* or *revealed* limit, but also that which is actually *without* a limit...

'In the same way, the Latin-speaking theologians of the early centuries abhorred what was indefinite, or liable to be misunderstood. Speculation they shunned and banned. The statements of the Creeds which issued forth from the early Roman Church are noted for their extreme brevity. The requisite facts were stated in black and white so that there might be no dubiety as to what people must believe. Roman Law, and the Roman military power, functioned like machines-authority must be obeyed. So in the Roman Church individualism of thought was not encouraged. As there was much speculation concerning the eons and the future, the position must needs be stated categorically and dogmatically.. If no one was able to chart the ocean of time, why not simply declare that it was boundless? Would not the Church wield far more power if it proclaimed in authoritative terms that eternal destiny was fixed here on earth?...'

TERTULLIAN

'At this point we must turn to Carthage in North Africa, and in particular to Tertullian, and take careful note of their profound and lasting influence over Christendom. Tertullian lived from about 160 to 220 A.D. Born at Carthage, he became a well-read scholar, an attractive orator and writer, a keen controversialist, and a clever lawyer. What Origen was, about the same period, to Greek or Eastern Christianity, Tertullian was to Latin or Western Christianity. He was the first one to set about systematically to explain the Scriptures in the Latin tongue of North Africa, and the first theologian to establish a technical Latin terminology for Christianity. It is no exaggeration to say that the choice of terms of this Latin scholar has profoundly affected all succeeding theological thought...

'Up till his time Roman Christianity had been essentially Greek in form, but when he embraced it, Latin terms and thoughts were introduced, which gradually but steadily altered the whole character of its teaching, and paved the way for the Roman Catholic system of dogma...

'Being well trained in Roman law he looked on God much more as the Judge who gives the law and must be obeyed, than as the Father of all. All relations between God and man partake of the nature of legal transactions, and thus a good act by man brings satisfaction to God and merit to man. But the fundamental relationship is that of fear on man's part. The great difference between the Greek Church and the Latin Church consisted in this, that the Greek Church looked upon revelation as expressing *God in His relation to man,* while the Latin Church began with man, and saw primarily *man as in relation to God*. God's measureless love and grace were viewed as at the disposal of man, or man was viewed as the fallen and guilty rebel measured up before the Judge. The one commenced with God and His love.. [t]he other saw man as on probation, and God as the magistrate...

'It was reserved for three great Carthaginians, Tertullian, Cyprian, and Augustine, so to influence the Latin Church that it deflected and declined into a system of dogmatic hierarchy.. It has been said that Tertullian often makes use of words not found in general use outside of the very early writers, and that he often imparts to words a new or unusual force...

This, then, is the man in the hollow of whose hands lay the clay which was to be moulded into concrete Latin dogma. This is the man in whose hands reclined the fate of the word *eternal*. What meaning did he give to it?...

'Augustine, who later outdid Tertullian and his doctrines, maintained that the whole human race was "one damned batch and mass of perdition"*(conspersis damnata, massa perditionis)*, out of which a few are elected to salvation, while all the remainder are lost for ever. He beheld evil as a force integral in a universe apart from God, while Origen believed that all is out from God, even evil, which God must undo and banish.

HOW THE OLD VERSIONS RENDERED AION

'The Old Syriac version is thought to have been made from the Greek about the end of the first century or some time during the second century. The language is closely akin to Hebrew, and was very like the Aramaic which was spoken in Palestine side by side with Greek in the first century. To translate the Greek eon and eonian it uses *olm*, which is exactly the word used in the Hebrew Scriptures, meaning "obscure," or "obscurity," that is, eonian and eon. The same constructions as occur in the Greek are shown, such as, from the eon *mn olm*, for the eon *l-olm*, this eon, that eon, for the eons to come, for the eon of the eons *l-olm olmin*, the conclusion of the eons.

'To prove that *olm* did not and could not stand for eternity, it may be stated that the Greek word *kosmos*(world) is generally rendered in the Syriac version by *olm*, as in John 1:10 (thrice), John 17:24, where the Syriac has, "preceding the disruption of the eon." The Syriac Version knew nothing about an eternity, and nothing in it is called eternal.

'The ancient Gothic version is of peculiar interest to the English-speaking and German-speaking peoples. In it are preserved the sole relies of a Germanic tongue spoken round 350 A.D., which was very closely akin to the old German and old English spoken about that time. It was translated direct from the Greek, although only fragments have survived, mostly of the New Testament. It is a very faithful and literal rendering, and at times even reproduces the pronunciation of Greek words, where these are transliterated. Needless to say, being entirely free from the influence of Jerome's Latin version, it does not contain Latin terms such as perish, damnation, perdition, torment, eternal, punishment. It uses exclusively what were then native German words, very simple and elementary. The Gothic is the first rendering of the Scriptures into any Teutonic tongue. The Goths were a very virile people from the North of Europe, who dominated most of Europe about the time this version was produced by Wulfila. Spreading southwards, they overran Greece and Italy, and captured Rome in 410 A.D. Eventually they seem to have died out of the Mediterranean countries, and as a distinct people they became lost to history.

'To show how close Gothic comes to modern English, it may be pointed out that the following words are either spelt or sounded exactly the same in each: all, arm, blind, brother, corn, daughter, door, dumb, finger, full, grass, hand, heart, hard, lamb, land, light, little, lust, while, white, year, young.

'The Coptic version, made probably about the end of the second century, for use in Egypt, and still used there, appears to render the Hebrew *olm* and the Greek *aion* by *eneh*, a word which is defined in Coptic dictionaries as meaning nothing more than "time."

'The Armenian version is ascribed to Mesrop (354-441 A.D.) and others. Conybeare says it "fits the Greek of the Septuagint as a glove the hand that wears it; keeping so close to the Greek that it has almost the same value for us as the Greek text itself, from which the translator worked, would possess."..

'The Ethiopic version, in the semitic language formerly spoken in Abyssinia, is thought to have been made in the fourth or fifth century, from the Greek. It reproduces the usual Greek expressions containing eon. The word used is *olm*, exactly the same as in Hebrew and Syriac. In Jude 25 it reads, "and for all the eons" *u-l-kul olmth*, showing the plural form. In Heb.9:26 it reads, "at the conclusion of the eon" (l-chlqth olm). In Eph.3:21 it reads, "in every generation and for the eon of the eon" *b-kl-thuld u-l-olm olm)*. In the Psalms it has a few times, as in 45:17, 48:14, and 52:8, "for the eon and for the eon of the eon" *l-olm, u-l-olm olm*. That this word *olm* assuredly could not signify "eternity" is placed beyond all doubt by the fact that it is also used to represent the Greek word for world (kosmos) generally, as throughout John 17. It also stands for the Greek word for era *kairos*, as in Mark 10:30 and Luke 18:30, and even for generation*genea* as in Luke 16:8.

'Old English versions were made not from the Greek, but from the Latin Vulgate, between the years 680 and 995. The four Gospels were done, and probably other parts. The Latin adjective *aeternum* (which Jerome used for eonian) is always rendered by the little word *ece*. Where Jerome for the noun has*seculum*, the Old English uses *worulde* (world) in all sixteen cases. Where Jerome has *in aeternum*, the Old English eight times has *ecnysse*, five times *never* (with a negative in the Latin), and once *ever*. The two words, *ece* and *world*, will amply repay a little investigation.

'The once very common English word *ece*, which can be traced down till about 1260 (although it disappeared as an adjective soon after that), is stated to come from the Old English verb *ecan*, meaning to "prolong, augment, increase." The word survives as a verb, to eke, meaning to add, lengthen, and as an adverb, meaning, also, in addition. A nickname was originally "an eke name," that is, an added name. In Scottish Law, an eik is an addition to a legal document.

'The reason why the simple word *ece* was forced out of English probably was that it was too equivocal. Theology was trying to make it stand for "everlasting," whereas it only meant "lasting." These latter terms were to take its place, as in Cursor Mundi (The Course of the World, a metrical version of Bible history, written about 1320), which has the line, "Through Jesus come to life lasting" (Thoru Jhesu com to liif lastand). Soon after this time, the word everlasting took the place of *ece* and *lasting*, a transition which made a very great deal of difference...

'It might here be remarked that an extraordinary change was going on in English speech between the twelfth and the fourteenth centuries. Up till the year 950 there was very little admixture of Latin or Danish words. The result of the Danish invasion meant that thousands of fine old poetic words became lost. From 1200 to 1280 was the most disastrous of all periods. A great many prose words disappeared, and the upper classes discarded English for French. For about eighty years after 1280 there was a vast inroad of French words to take the place of English words driven out of circulation, or forced to become merely dialectal. From about 1360 a new standard of English was spoken at Court, and French ceased to be fashionable. It was what has been described as this "wild anarchy of speech" that was raging in England from 1300 to 1500 that caused many words to take on new meanings or lose their old meanings. These facts have been noted briefly merely because of their connection with John Wiclif, and so that we may understand more clearly his usage of the word world."

WICLIF AND HIS VERSION

'John Wiclif was probably the first person to translate the whole Bible into the English tongue. He was born about 1320, at the time when the language of England was in the melting-pot. He commenced by translating the Unveiling in 1356, and, with the help of collaborators, finished the entire Bible by 1382. Two years later he died. Well did he live up to one of his sayings, that "Christian men ought to travail night and day about text of holy writ." He is noteworthy as having been described as the one Englishman who during the past eleven hundred years was able to mold Christian thought on the continent of Europe. Not only was his private life irreproachable, but in his opposition to the claims of the Roman Church he was without fear of any man. In addition, he was a true scholar, and wrote a great many books, mostly in Latin. These became very popular in Bohemia (now part of the modern Czecho-Slovakia), as King Richard II of England had married the devout Princess Anne of Bohemia, a lover of the Scriptures. While at Prague university, John Huss came under the influence of Wiclif's writings, and in 1415 he was burnt at the stake for his faith. The followers of Huss became very numerous, and long-continued wars against them failed to extirpate them. Their powerful influence spread to the neighboring parts of Germany, including Saxony, where Martin Luther was born, who became a fearless champion of the Scriptures.

'The Latin Vulgate version dominated Europe for the thousand years which lay between Jerome and Wiclif, and longer. No one seems to have thought in those times of a Greek original, and in any case, the Greek language was all but forgotten in Europe. The Catholic Church used Latin in its services, and Latin had displaced Greek completely as the universal language of courts and clergy and scholars. It will therefore be of great interest to observe how Wiclif rendered the Latin of the Vulgate, and to note his views concerning the future. We shall find that his language differs markedly from that used by the various translations which were made from the time of Tyndale, one hundred and fifty years after Wiclif, including Coverdale's (1535), Cranmer's (1539), the Genevan (1557), and the Rheims (1582), down to the Authorized of 1611. Never once does Wiclif use the expression "for ever," or "for ever and ever." Though he uses "everlasting," he never uses "eternal." Had the Authorized Version been the next English version to be made after Wiclif's it would never have found acceptance. As it was, it enjoyed the benefit of following closely on the lines of a number of fairly similar versions, which thus paved the way for it. Though the expressions used by Wiclif are far from perfect, great is the decline manifested in the next English version to be published, Tyndale's. Tyndale brought in "for ever," "for ever and ever," "for evermore," where

Wiclif expressed no such thought. Instead of the Reformation and the revival of learning bringing in added light regarding the times to come, they brought about gross darkness and confusion.

'As has been stated, Wiclif used "world" to represent the Latin *seculum*, which Jerome used for the Greek *aion*..

'Wiclif, it would seem, came near to restoring a great truth to its proper place. Had he had the Greek text before him, there is little doubt that he would have accomplished this. As it was, the inconsistency of the Latin Vulgate obliged him also to be somewhat inconsistent, and this may be the reason why versions which came after his time most unfortunately used "world" in a sense different from his usage. By Tyndale's time, world had come to be used as meaning a state or place, rather than a limited period of time.

In his "Synonyms of the New Testament," Archbishop Trench draws a contrast between *kosmos* (world) and *aion* (eon), both of which are rendered in the Authorized Version by "world." In the case of *aion* he thinks more use might have been made of "age." He regrets that the translators did not somehow mark the difference between *kosmos* (mundus), the world contemplated under aspects of space, and *aion*(seculum), the same contemplated under aspects of time, as Latin, like Greek, has two distinct words, where we have, or have acted as though we had, but one. In a note he shows that the word "world," etymologically regarded, more nearly represents *aion* than *kosmos*. Our old word *weorulde* is composed of two distinct parts, and where the primitive pronunciation is preserved, two very distinct syllables are still heard. The former part of the word consists of wer, a man (like the Latin *vir*, as in virile, and the *-er* in words like speaker, also the wer- in werwolf, the man-wolf). The latter part of the word is *ald*, or *elde*, meaning age or generation. World is therefore defined as "the generation of men." That there is a close connection between the old word world and "eon" was beautifully shown by the old Gothic version, which, in 2 Tim.4: 10 has, for "this present world" (C.V. "the current eon"), the reading, *tho nu ald*, meaning, "this now age."

Quite apart from the manner in which Wiclif translated the Scriptures, however, we are not left in any doubt as to his views regarding future time. Among his voluminous works in Latin, there is one called Trialogus, or a discussion between three parties, whom he calls Truth, Liar, and Prudence. This contains a dissertation on the distinction between eternity, eons, and time, extending to over a thousand words. He says, "It is one matter for a thing to exist always, and another for a thing to be eternal; the world exists always, because at every time, and yet it is not eternal, because it is created, for the moment of creation must have a beginning, as the world had."'

'The Reformation, which was a reformation along certain lines only, instead of undoing and reversing this grievous error of the Latin Church, actually confirmed it and established it. On the other hand, every ancient version of the Scriptures, and every modern or medieval translation, either by its consistency where it is consistent, or by its inconsistency, proves the CONCORDANT VERSION to be correct in its renderings of the words under examination. Every translation which does not consistently use the words "eon" and "eonian," or "age" and "age-abiding," or some such terms, is obliged to make use of at least two mutually contradictory expressions.

Verily indeed, it is a strong claim which we make on behalf of the CONCORDANT VERSION, but we make it without fear of its being refuted, and without fear of any opposition, that it is the only version, which, *by its system, adequately recognizes* the Scriptures as God-breathed.

This article was originally serialized in Unsearchable Riches magazine (Vol. 26, Nos. 5 & 6, Sept. and Nov. 1935). They were later reprinted in book form, with some alterations from this text, under the title "Whence Eternity?"

BIBLIOGRAPHY

1.   Many of the stories in opening chapters presented here are adapted from old jokes and fables from memory or casual exchange. I couldn't possibly recall exactly where I came across many of these anecdotes and tales, so full disclosure, I put my own literary touch on some of these old yarns and folktales as segue into substance.

2. *The Problem of Pain*- C.S. Lewis (HarperOne, San Francisco: 1940), 129.

3.   *The Fire That Consumes*- Edward William Fudge (Verdict Publications: 1982), 419,420.

4.   The Economist magazine: December 2012.

5.   See also: 1 Sa 28.13-14; Jn 20.17; He 9.15; 1 Pt 3.19; 4.5-6.

6. *A Mighty Fortress is our God*—Martin Luther (lyrics, music andMIDI file at Cyber Hymnal).

7.   See: Js 15.8; 18.16; Ne 11.30; Je 7.30-32; 32.35.

8.   See: 2 Ki 16.1-3; 21.1-6; 2 Chr 33.1-6.

9.   *Erasing Hell*- Francis Chan & Preston Sprinkle (David C. Cook Distribution, Ontario, Canada: 2011), 89.

10.   KJV Life in the Spirit Study Bible (Zondervan, Grand Rapids, MI: 1992), 1151.

11.   2 Ki 25.3; La 4.4,5,9.

12.   *The Bible Unearthed: Archeology's New Vision of Ancient Israel and the Origin of Its Sacred Texts*- Finkelstein & Silberman (Simon & Schuster: 2001).

Clay ostraca referred to as the Lachish letters from this period were discovered during excavations; one, which was probably written to the commander at Lachish from an outlying base, describes how the signal fires from nearby towns are disappearing: *'And may (my lord) be apprised that we are watching for the fire signals of Lachish according to all the signs which my lord has given, because we cannot see Azeqah'.*[14] This correlates with the book of Jeremiah,[15] which states that Jerusalem, Lachish and Azekah were the last cities to fall to the Babylonians. Archaeological finds from Jerusalem testify that virtually the whole city within the walls was burnt to rubble in 587 BCE and utterly destroyed.[10]:295

Finkelstein, Israel; Silberman, Neil Asher (2001). The Bible Unearthed: Archaeology's New Vision of Ancient Israel and the Origin of Its Sacred Texts. Simon and

Schuster. ISBN 978-0-684-86912-4

13. The International Bible Commentary, 2nd Edition (Zondervan, Grand Rapids, MI: 1986), 64.

14. *The Fire That Consumes*, 185.

And Josephus wrote, 'Now the next day was the festival of Xylophory; upon which the custom was for every one to bring wood for the altar that there never be a want of fuel for that fire which is unquenchable and always burning'. –The Wars of the Jews- Flavius Josephus, William Whiston (translator); http://www.creationism.org/books/josephus/index.htm

15. www.centuryone.org/essene.html

16. Josephus- Wars vi. 8, #5 v 12, #7.

17. *Raising Hell*- Julie Ferwerda (Vagabond Group, Lander, WY: 2011), 49.

18. Ibid, 49.

19. *On the Reasonableness of Christianity*- John Locke, cited in *The Conditionalist Faith of our Fathers*- Edwin LeRoy Froom (Review & Herald Publishing Assn., Washington D.C.: 1965) Vol. 2; 188.

20. Daniel 12.2-3 in the Hebrew interlinear:

'u·rbim and·many-ones מ ֽ ֭ י ׁ֣ש ֵ ֗נ ִ֥י m·ishni from·sleepers-of א ָ֖ד ֥ מ ַ֑ת admth ground-of ־

- ֖ ע ֔פ ר ophr soil ֗יק ִ֣י צוּ iqitzu they-shall-cawake א ֥ ל ֗ ה ale these ֗ ל ֥ ח ֽ יֵ ֖ל·chii

to·lives-of ל ֑ ֖ ע ם oulm eon And many of them that sleep in the dust of the earth shall

awake, some to everlasting life, and some to shame [and] everlasting contempt. 2 ֖ 1, א ֥

ה ֥ ל u·ale and·these ֗ ל ֥ ח ֑ ר פ ַ֖ת l·chrphuth to·the·reproaches ֑ ל ֗ ד ֥ ר א ַ֖ן l·draun

to·repulsion-of ל ֑ ֖ ע ם oulm eon : : ס s'

21.   Somewhere between about 604-585 B.C., Edom seems to have fallen out of favor with the Empire. We notice that Edom isn't

mentioned as an ally of Nebuchadnezzar when they go in to crush Judah (2 Ki 24.1-2).

'[B]y the fifth century Arab names had appeared at Ezion-geber. In the Persian period the land of Edom had no sedentary occupation. The Edomites were displaced by nomadic Arab tribes.' (The Books of Joel, Obadiah, Jonah, and Micah, L. C. Allen, NICOT, p130, 1976 AD)

http://www.bible.ca/archeology/bible-archeology-edomite-territory-mt-seir.htm#IV

Also see 1 Esdras 3:1-4:63.

Like the prophecies in the book of Obadiah (written about 585 B.C.), these were unbelievable predictions! It would be like predicting that everyone in Los Angeles will be killed and that Southern California will become uninhabited except for wild animals—*while the rest of the United States continues normally!*

Clarifying Christianity comments, 'The history books tell us that Edom did OK for perhaps a hundred years after their final warning from God's prophets. Then, during the fifth century (400-499) B.C. the "Edomites" were overwhelmed by other Arab groups. In turn, these groups were taken over by the Nabataeans, who started living in the area sometime around 312 B.C. By the way, the Nabataeans, not the Edomites, are the people who cut the temples in the sandstone walls of Petra.[1] Under the Nabataeans, the city of Petra flourished until 106 A.D., when the Romans conquered Petra.[2] From that time it slid into disuse, to the point that Edom was almost uninhabited from the 7th to the 12th century A.D. It revived slightly in the 12th century when the crusaders built a castle there called Sel. Afterward, it remained so forgotten that it had to be rediscovered in 1812 by Swiss traveler Johann.' L. Burckhardt.[3]: http://www.clarifyingchristianity.com/fulfill.shtml

[1]Thompson, J.A. (1962) *The Bible and Archaeology* Wm. B. Eerdmans Publishing Co., Grand Rapids, Michigan p. 232,233

[2]Millard, Alan (1985) *Treasures From Bible Times*, Lion Publishing pic, Oxford, England, p. 60-63.

[3]Encyclopedia Britannica, 13/xvii-751

John Calvin also weighs in, 'The prophet's language is undoubtedly hyperbolical... When he declares that the wrath of God against the Edomites will resemble a fire of God that burns continually, he cuts off from them all hope of pardon'.

www.ccel.org/.../**calvin**/calcom15.iii.i....

Jamiesson, Faucett & Brown finally point out, 'Edom's original offense was: they would not let Israel pass through their land in peace to Canaan: God recompenses them in kind, no traveller shall pass through Edom. Volney, the infidel, was forced to confirm the truth of this prophecy: "From the reports of the Arabs, southeast of the Dead Sea, within three days' journey are upwards of thirty ruined towns, absolutely deserted."' Jamiesson, Faucett & Brown. *A Commentary Critical, Practical & Explanatory of the Old & New Testaments- Volume II.* Toledo, OH: Jerome B. Names & Co. 1884.196.

22. www.ccel.org/.../**calvin**/calcom15.iii.i.....

23. See also: 2 Ki 19.30; Jb 18.16; Is 11.1; 53.2.

24. *The Moral Compass*- William Bennett (Simon & Schuster, New York, NY: 1995), 224.

25. *Erasing Hell*- Chan, 52.

26. www.hiddenbible.com/**enoch/online**.html..

27. wesley.nnu.edu/.../noncanonical-literature......

28. Ibid.

29. Ibid.

30. Ibid.

31. More apocryphal passages on 'hell' include 1 Enoch 53.3; 56.1; 62.11; 63.1-7; 90.26,27; 91.9-14; 103.5-8; 108.3,4; 2 Enoch 10.2; 40.13; L.A.B. 16.3; 23.6; 2 Baruch 44.15; 59.5-12; 4 Ezra 7.38,80,82; T. Zeb. 10.3; Wis. 4.14,15; 1 QS 4.11-14.

32. *The Moral Compass*- Bennett, 331.

33. Mt 13.42; 24.51; Lk 13.28.

34. Jb 16.9; Ps 35.19; 37.12; La 2.16; Ac 7.54.

35. *The Fire That Consumes*- Fudge, 178 citing *The Righteous Judge: A Study of the Biblical Doctrine   of Everlasting Punishment*- Harold E. Guillebaud (Taunton, Great Britain: Phoenix Press, n.d.).

36. *Auntient Lere, a Selection of Aphoristical and Preceptive Passages from the Works of Eminent English Authors*. London. Printed by J. Barfield, Wardour-Street; for Longman, Hurst, Rees, Orme & Brown; Paternoster-Row; Rodwell, New Bond-Street; Setchell, King-Street, Covent-Garden, and Finsbury-Place, 1812.65.

37. *Raising Hell*- Julie Ferwerda (Vagabond Group, Lander, WY: 2011), 49.

38. Isaiah 65.20, 'There shall be no more thence an infant of days, nor an old man that hath not filled his days: for the child shall die an hundred years old; but the sinner being an hundred years old shall be accursed.'

39. 1 Th 4.15; see also: Ac 7.60; 1 Co 15.6, 18; 1 Th 4.13; 2 Pt 3

40.   Erasing Hell- Chan, 98.

41. Re 2.11; 20.6,14; 21.8.

42.   *The Final Prophecy of Jesus*- Professor Oral Edward Collins (Wipf & Stock Publishers, Eugene, OR: 2007), 334.

43. 1 Th 2.9; 3.10; see also: Ac 9.24; Re 12.10.

44. Re 13.11-17; 16.13; 19.20.

45. *The Fire That Consumes*, Fudge, 303.

46.   Ibid, 416.

47.   *Raising Hell*- Ferwerda, 53.

48.   Ibid, 55.

49.   thetencommandmentsministry.us/ministry/free_bible/**whence_eternity.**

'It was the Emperor Justinian in A.D. 533 that gave much greater force to Stephen's ancient order, waning. Justinian's Decree, aka Emperor Justinian's Imperial Law, asserted the absolute supremacy of the Bishop, It appears, *over all men*, Christian or not. Warlords and kings alike were realizing that this man of the cloth might like the feel of a crown, and could now just as easily hold political sway over them.

'But time has a way of relaxing the attention. Absolute deference was not being paid to the Supreme Pontiff, and 'the decree was enforced by arms, and the title *Rector Ecclesiae*, or 'Lord of the Church' was bestowed (D'Aubigne's *Reformation*, Vol. I, p. 42).' 'Vigilius ascended the papal chair in 538 A.D. under the *military* protection of Belisarius' (Hist. Of the Chr. Church, Vol. 3, p. 327). Essentially, there was now a military arm of the Roman Church, and fidelity *by force* was now the official policy. * cited from my commentary on Matthew 24- *The Vulture that Plucked Out the Sun*; p. 45.

50. *Raising Hell*, Ferwerda, 132 .

51. Ibid, 128.

52. Ibid, 128.

53. Ibid, 128.

54. *Christ Alone*- Michael E. Wittmer (Edenridge Press, Grand Rapids, MI: 2011), 64.

55. *Raising Hell*- Ferwerda, 131.

56. Ibid, 131.

57. www.tentmaker.org/tracts/Does**ForeverS**.html.

58. *The Fire That Consumes*- Fudge, 200 citing *The Works of Jonathan Edwards*, 2:515-525.

59. Ibid, 201 cited with reference by White, *Life in Christ*, p.xi; and Froom, *Conditionalist Faith*,2:220.

60. Ibid, 201 citing Froom- *Conditionalist Faith*, 2:797.

61. Ibid, 387, 388 citing John Milton, *Paradise Lost*, bk. 10,11.789-793, also cited by Froom- *Conditionalist Faith*, 2:156.

62. Ibid, 389.

63. Ibid, 57.

64. See also: Mt12.32; Ep 1.21; 1 Ti 4.8; He 6.5

65. Jb 22.15-17; Ps 5.5,23;; 9.17; 37.1-2, 22,38; 139.19; Pr 5.21-23; 10.27; 11.19; 14.12; Ezk 3.19; 18.4,20; Mt 7.13; 25.30; Lk 12.20; Jn 3.15-20, 36; 5.29; 8.21, 24; Ac 24.15; Ro 9.22; He

10.27; Re 20.13.

66. *The Fathers of the Church: Augustine. The City of God. Books XVII-XXII.* The Catholic University of America Press: Washington D.C.: 1954.369.

67. *The Fire That Consumes-* Fudge, 269 as cited by Edward White- *Life in Christ,* 365.

68. Mt 8.10-12; 22.11-13; 25.14-30; Lk 12.35-48

69. *All That God Has For You-* Dr. Ken Baker. Elim Ministries Publishing; 22 The Haven, Roscrea, Co. Tipperary, Ireland. 2015: citing Munch, 19.

70. Ex 12.24; 29.9; 40.15; Lv 3.17; 1 Ki 8.12,13; 2 Ki 5.27; Dt 23.3,6.

71. *The Problem of Immortality-* Emmanuel Petavel (Eliot Stock, London: 1892; translated by Frederick Ash Freer from the French), 574.
See also: Ps 40.5,12a, 'Many, O LORD my God, are thy wonderful works which thou hast done, and thy thoughts which are to us-ward: they cannot be reckoned up in order unto thee: if I would declare and speak of them, they are more than can be numbered... For innumerable evils have compassed me about'.

72. thetencommandmentsministry.us/ministry/free_bible/**whence_eternity**.

73. Ibid.

74. Ibid.

75. Ibid.

76. Ibid.

77. Ibid.

78. Ibid.

79. Also, just a reminder; a reread of subsection 'ORDERS STRAIGHT FROM THE TOP' from chapter 11 may be helpful as we have reexamined this matter of 'ages', as opposed to eternity.

80. *A Boy Called It-* Dave Pelzer (Health Communications, Inc., Deerfield Beach, FL: 1995).

81. *What's the Truth About Heaven and Hell?* Jacoby, Douglas A.: Eugene, Oregon: Harvest House Publishers, 2013.105.

82. *The Liberty of Man, Woman & Child-* Robert G. Ingersoll (Kessinger Publishing, Whitefish, MO: 2005- reprinted from original *Liberty For All*: 1877).

83. *The Problem of Immortality-* Petavel, 267.

84. *The Inescapable Love of God-* Thomas Talbott (Universal Publishers: 1999), 140-152.

85. *The Destruction of the Finally Impenitent-* Clark H. Pinnock (McMaster Divinity College

THE SLUMS of HEAVEN

Hamilton, Ontario, CA) cited in *Conditional Immortality*- Barry, 55,56.

Made in USA - Kendallville, IN
1085720_9798601314213
04.22.2020 0946